Preface to the Second Printing

In March 2009 President Obama signed into law the Omnibus Public Lands Management Act, which included permanent protection for nearly two million acres of America's wild places. A hefty chunk of that total—428,000 acres—now preserves several very special Eastern Sierra bioregions.

Doff your hats to the many national and California conservation organizations and local groups who worked hard to preserve these extraordinary, pristine landscapes, and to President Obama, Senator Barbara Boxer and Representative Buck McKeon for getting the bill passed. They leave a priceless legacy for future generations to enjoy, as well as an intact landscape for innumerable species of flora and fauna.

Among the additions germane to this hiking guide: Hoover Wilderness has 79,820 acres of newly designated wilderness, Ansel Adams Wilderness has 528 new acres, Owens River Headwaters Wilderness has 14,721 new acres, White Mountain Wilderness has a whopping 229,993 new acres, and John Muir Wilderness has 70,411 added acres.

As defined by the original Wilderness Act of 1964, a wilderness area is a section of publicly owned land "where the earth and its community of life are untrammeled by man, where man himself is a visitor who does not remain." Wilderness boundaries appear to most of us as just lines on a map, but to the plants and animals who can't live anywhere else, the lines are very real because they demarcate a safe zone.

Inside the lines Americans have decided that these precious lands will forever remain affected primarily by the forces of nature with the human imprint substantially unnoticeable. Within the lines people can return year after year without fear of finding a parking lot, rows of condominiums, or other real estate developments.

Thanks to the perseverance and diligence of countless wilderness warriors that led to passage of the Omnibus Public Lands Act, nearly a half million more Eastern Sierra acres can now allow Mother Nature to continue to do what she does best. This great victory for wilderness and its inhabitants makes our book even better than when we created it in 2005.

Sharon Giacomazzi
July 2009

One touch of nature makes the whole world kin.
~ William Shakespeare

Exploring
Eastern Sierra Canyons

SONORA PASS TO PINE CREEK

Hiking ◆ *Backpacking*
Rustic Resorts ◆ *History*
Camping ◆ *Picnicking*
Wildflowers & Autumn Color
Horseback Riding & Pack Stations

Sharon Giacomazzi

BORED FEET PRESS
MENDOCINO, CALIFORNIA
2009

Cover Photograph, *Fall colors along McGee Creek* by Claude Fiddler
Back cover photograph by Paul McFarland
Maps by Marsha Mello
Edited by Donna Bettencourt & Bob Lorentzen
Cover & book design by Elizabeth Petersen
Composition by Wendy Blakeway of DesignXperts
Bighorn sheep illustration by Amber Brandauer

Published and Distributed by
    Bored Feet Press
    www.boredfeet.com
    Post Office Box 1832
    Mendocino, CA 95460
    (707)964-6629, (888)336-6199

Cataloging-in-Publication Data
Giacomazzi, Sharon
Exploring eastern Sierra canyons: Sonora Pass to Pine Creek: hiking • backpacking • rustic resorts • history • camping • picnicking • wildflowers & autumn color • horseback riding & pack stations
        p. cm.
Includes bibliographical references (p.) and index.
ISBN 978-0-939431-32-8

10 9 8 7 6 5 4 3 2   ISBN 978-0-939431-32-8

Dedication

Dedicated to my steadfast trail companions L.A.P. and Cosie and to those special people who sparked my love affair with the high, wild places in the Sierra Nevada. This book is also dedicated to Eastern Sierra visitors in the hope they will enjoy the magnificent canyon journeys, and respect its majestic, irreplaceable landscape and all its inhabitants, plant and animal, with whom we share life on Planet Earth.

Life is not measured by the number of breaths we take, but by the moments that take our breath away.

~Anonymous

Acknowledgments

Thank you my dear Sierra hiking friends who contributed in ways great and small to the birth of this book. For your generous gifts of time, enthusiasm, energy and encouragement, I am profoundly grateful. I will always honor your assistance.

In particular, I offer thanks to Lois Perry, Tom Wieg, Michele Minniear, Anna Meacham, Karen Stern, Lynn Robertson, Paul McFarland, Joan Conlan, Amber Brandauer, and Inyo and Humboldt-Toiyabe National Forest personnel. Bob Lorentzen and Donna Bettencourt, publisher and editor extraordinaire, I salute you.

Contents

Illustrations

continued on page 184

Foreword

by Ardeth Huntington
Author of *Yosemite: A Personal Discovery*

In choosing a subject to capture the imagination of readers who were enriched by her first book, *Trails and Tales of Yosemite and the Central Sierra*, Sharon Giacomazzi followed her heart eastward from Yosemite across the 14,000-foot summits of the Sierra mountains to a region that Sierra aficionados label simply—but with heartfelt fondness—"The East Side."

For some, fondness spills over into passion, and that is what you will find in Sharon's writing. Her love of exploring High Country wilderness is evident in her detailed research and in the enthusiastic descriptions of terrain she knows and loves. But you will find more than well-crafted word pictures in these pages. You will recognize that her motive in writing this book is to entice you, to put you under the spell of Eastern Sierra canyons, regions you may have driven near, fingered on a map, or felt intrigued by, hearing a Yosemite enthusiast declare as Sierra snows melt into spring, "I can hardly wait to get over to the East Side!"

By crossing Yosemite National Park's eastern boundaries into a region so stunningly different from Yosemite, Sharon has chosen to introduce to explorers, hikers, in fact to all travelers, a comparatively unused landscape, often seen as barren, but in fact a region of profound gorges offering a feast of nature's riches. In these pages, you'll find the key to on-trail experiences, while you explore High Sierra terrain you perhaps felt was not easily accessible, or mountainsides that from an automobile window failed to reveal their secluded beauty. You will find in this book guides to hiking in spectacular canyon landscapes that are best explored on foot.

If you are curious about the east side of the Sierra, this book will get you there—especially if you are a person who can't wait to lace up boots, tuck in a water bottle and some trail snacks and set off for these backcountry destinations following Sharon's thoughtfully explicit guidelines. Armchair adventurers will also share in the pleasure of her journeys with every turn of a page.

Sharon's affinity for Robert Frost's suggestion to "take the road less traveled" is borne out in her encouragement that you become, with the help of this book, an east side explorer. As Frost implies, " . . . it may make all the difference."

The Eastern Sierra: Walker to Bishop

Walker

TO TOPAZ LAKE AND RENO

SONORA PASS 9624'

108

TO SONORA

395

WEST WALKER

DEVIL'S GATE SUMMIT 7519'

Sweetwater

WALKER LAKE

95

Hawthorne

LITTLE WALKER RIVER

BUCKEYE ROAD

395

BUCKEYE CREEK

182

BRIDGE-PORT LAKE

Masonic

HOOVER

WILDERNESS

TWIN LAKES ROAD

Bridgeport

UPPER TWIN LAKE

LOWER TWIN LAKE

GREEN CRK. RD.

Bodie

Aurora

270

359

YOSE-MITE

VIRGINIA LAKES RD.

CONWAY SUMMIT 8138'

LUNDY LK. RD.

SADDLEBAG LAKE

LUNDY LAKE

NEGIT ISLAND

167

NEVADA

CALIFORNIA

TUOLUMNE MEADOWS

Lee Vining

MONO

PAOHA ISLAND

TIOGA PASS 9945'

120

395

LAKE

NATIONAL

PARK

ANSEL

GRANT LAKE

SILVER LAKE

120

ADAMS

158

JUNE LAKE

DEADMAN SUMMIT 8041'

JUNE MOUNTAIN

WILDERNESS

OWENS RIVER

DEVIL'S POSTPILE NATL. MON.

Mammoth Lakes

203

395

MAMMOTH MTN.

120

6

BENTON HOT SPRINGS

Benton

SHERWIN CREEK RD.

JOHN

CONVICT LAKE

CONVICT LK. RD.

LAKE CROWLEY

MUIR

McGEE CREEK RD.

Tom's Place

WILDERNESS

ROCK CREEK RD.

SHERWIN SUMMIT 7000'

OWENS

N

ROCK CREEK LAKE

395

PINE CREEK RD.

RIVER

6

0   5   10   15

MILES

TO BIG PINE, INDEPENDENCE AND LONE PINE

Bishop

Introduction

I invite you to celebrate a magnificent landscape just west of Highway 395 between Sonora Pass Junction and Bishop. This guidebook offers trail descriptions and intriguing historical information to entice you to explore twenty-five dramatically beautiful canyons that cleave the towering granite ramparts of the Eastern Sierra Nevada escarpment. These canyons, as well as those farther south to Lone Pine, are inarguably a hiker's paradise. Good trails thread ancient glacial corridors teeming with wild, incomparable scenery.

The Eastern Sierra, of course, encompasses the entire 400-mile length of the range, but its quintessence lies in the roughly 125-mile stretch between Lone Pine and Sonora Pass. Compared to the long, gentle upward rise on the western slope, the east side is abruptly steep; only a few thousand feet separate crest from valley. The region is sliced by stupendous U-shaped gashes watered by snowmelt streams racing down the precipitous scarp to the high desert far below. With a few exceptions, the trails are steep.

The sunrise side of John Muir's beloved "Range of Light" is a region of lavish beauty, astonishing biodiversity and extraordinary contrasts. The Eastern Sierra contains more diverse, dramatic mountain-desert scenery and natural wonders than any other location in North America. Within a relatively small area, you can find miles and miles of nonstop wild scenery of infinite variety. A rendezvous of hot springs, cinder cones, glaciers, and hundreds of lakes are the tip-off to once fierce geologic activity. Earthquake faults, tremors, fumaroles and active glaciers attest to ongoing geologic changes. Extremes abound in the bristlecone pines, which have been found to be the oldest living organisms on earth, in the craters of one of the youngest volcanic areas in the West, and in Mount Whitney, the highest mountain in the lower 48 states. World-class routes for hiking, climbing, skiing, and mountain biking are waiting for you to begin your adventure.

In my opinion, this outrageously beautiful interface of mountain-desert topography, climate, and geology, with its varied plant and animal communities, should be designated a national park. There is no other place like it on the planet.

Hiking in the stunning canyons carved by the actions of water and ice is a rich, rewarding, multilayered experience. Literally everywhere you turn there is something remarkable, something utterly breathtaking. Highway 395, one of the West's most scenic roads, hugs the base of the entire Eastern Sierra and provides easy access into the marvelous canyons to campsites and trailheads that lead deeper into the High Sierra and over stark alpine passes at the crest. Other roads probe the lonely desert to the east. Few travelers buzzing along this route that runs from the Mojave Desert to the Nevada border are aware of the spectacular scenery only a few miles away.

Because they're out of sight, it is indeed difficult for anyone to imagine the extravagances of nature hidden in the steep-sided gorges, home to lush, flowery meadows, chains of azure lakes, exuberant waterfalls and streams, vast pine and aspen forests, wide variety of animal life, dazzling fall color and the jaw-dropping, up close and personal presence of the mighty Sierra. Such an exquisite tapestry of alpine scenery in this highest and wildest part of the range is unexpected and startling in comparison to the subtle beige and gray tones and somber mood of the high desert environment along Highway 395. The Eastern Sierra is a powerful, bold landscape, one you're not likely to forget and one you'll be compelled to visit many times over. A life time of summers would not be enough to explore, understand and appreciate its complex character, immense scale and splendor.

Should you be hesitant to get your boots on rather vertical trails, it's time to adjust your thinking. Although it can be strenuous, sometimes challenging, Eastern Sierra hiking is more about attitude than altitude. Rethink your I-don't-know-if-I-can-do-it attitude so that the pleasure and satisfaction of reaching a goal is secondary to the sheer joy of moving amidst such spectacular and precious landscapes. In short, take one step at a time and stop worrying about steepness or how far and long you can manage. Rest when you're tired and turn around whenever you want. Keep in mind the old saw—the journey is the destination.

Like a packrat, I've gathered bits of this and that from my twenty-five years of hiking Eastern Sierra trails. Each trip adds more tidbits to a special cache of mountain treasures tucked away in my memory bank. From time to time, I take them out, dust them off and revisit the magnificent places where I found these bright little jewels during my rambles. My first and most precious memory is looking down into the colorful, awesome abyss of Lundy Canyon on fire with fall color. I recall standing on the rim, speechless and quiet as a stump, hardly able to take in such beauty.

In time, you, too, will gather your own shiny baubles to stash away in your treasure chest of memories. And they'll come in many shapes and sizes. Perhaps it will be a thunderstorm raging over the fanged peaks gnawing at the Sierra skyline, or a pudgy marmot snoozing on a rock or the dance of light and shadow deep within an aspen grove. Maybe it will be the time you forgot your lunch, or swam in a lake so blue it didn't seem of this earth, or when your teenage daughter high-fived you atop a 12,000-foot summit.

Something to remember: Your feet are like dogs—they're happiest when they're going somewhere. I've come to understand that nothing can take the place of being in the Eastern Sierra in person and on foot. Reading books or watching videos about it is enriching and informative, and you'll glean many fascinating facts. However, facts and statistics, no matter how amazing, do not come even close to the essence of the Eastern Sierra. Words are simply inadequate to describe its intrinsic character. A picture is truly worth a thousand words, including mine in this guide book.

If you really want to know about this unrivaled piece of California real estate, you must get out of the car and walk or ride a horse on some of the trails. To feel its pulse and know it with your heart, rather than your head, involves more than passively and quickly looking around in a canyon through the windshield or snapping a photo at a turnout.

I believe that each of us embraces a last, best place in our hearts—a part of the world that resonates with our energy, that creates a bond with nature and nurtures and restores our souls. When we find our spiritual home, we know instantly it is where we belong and can find peace and joy. For me, the Eastern Sierra is that best place for my soul, where I am "home" and where I feel truly alive.

In every walk with nature, one receives far more than he seeks.

~John Muir

How to Use this Book

The basic purpose of this book is to encourage you to explore the Eastern Sierra on foot, the very best mode of travel to make its acquaintance. It is my intent to lure first-time visitors out of their cars and onto the trails to experience the mountains on their own terms and in ways motorists will never know. Only pedestrians carry the key to unlock the infinitely rich treasures waiting to be discovered in Eastern Sierra wilderness. For those more familiar with the joys and rewards of trail walking, I hope to expand your knowledge and instill a deep appreciation for this exhilarating, wondrous landscape. By walking along backcountry paths you'll develop an intimate relationship and greater understanding of how the natural world works, how every single animate and inanimate thing has a place, value and function and is inextricably interconnected. More importantly, perhaps, you'll begin to discover and understand your place in the great web of life.

Although the focus of this book is on day hikes, all twenty-five outings lend themselves to backpacking trips. Except for a few of them, hikes are moderately strenuous to strenuous and trace steep trails at elevations between 7200 feet and 12,000 feet. One-third of the journeys begin at elevations above 9000 feet. All of the treks are suitable for adventurous and energetic novice or average hikers in good health who have a yen to explore nature's magnificent gifts in Eastern Sierra canyons. This book will help you select and plan an outing by offering detailed trail descriptions. Armchair travelers can enjoy vicarious backcountry tours and accompanying historical information. If you choose not to hike, motorists will discover many stunning, scenic surprises while driving into the canyons to trailheads at road's end. Sampling Eastern Sierra grandeur in this fashion may provide the spark to get your feet on a trail in the near future.

You'll find summary information at the beginning of each chapter. This overview outlines how to find the trailhead, nearby camping and lodging options, hike distance, difficulty rating, best time to go, cautions about hazards you may encounter or restrictions on use, starting and ending elevations, maps and where to get further information. What the book doesn't do is teach you how to hike or develop common sense. You must remember that guide books can neither completely alert you to every hazard or challenge you may face nor anticipate your capabilities and limitations. You alone must always be personally responsible for your own safety. Exercise good judgment and use common sense.

A word about rating a hike's difficulty: This is rather tricky because the ease or difficulty of any trek depends primarily on the hiker's fitness level. Other impor-

Map Legend

ⓣ	Trailhead
▬▬▬	Paved Road/ Hwy.
═══	Unpaved Road
=====	Unimproved Road
– – –	Described Trail
··········	Other Trail or cross-country route
～～	River/ Creek
·~··~··	Seasonal Creek
～	Waterfall
—·—·—	Park or Wilderness Boundry
ʌ	Summit/ Peak
◊	Spring
o—o	Gate
⇧	Lodging
⇑	Ranger Station
▲	Campground
□	Point of Interest
℗	Parking
⊰	Mine Site
⤬	Picnic Area

tant factors include adaptability to high elevation, heaviness of your pack, trail and weather conditions. As a rule, physical condition has little to do with age. There are lots of very fit senior citizens, and there are lots of 30-year-old couch potatoes. The bottom line is that none of these journeys should be a death march. There is no hiking rule that requires you to get to the end of the trail. You have full control over your pace and when and where you'll stop.

Besides stupendous scenery, the Sierra Nevada harbors countless intriguing tales from yesteryear. To make the journeys even more alluring and meaningful, each hike is accompanied by an historical account of the area it passes through.

At the heart of this book is the hope that, by enticing you to investigate unimaginable scenic and historic routes, you will realize the urgency and importance of protecting what remains of our natural world and cultural heritage. If one person like John Muir can make such a difference in preserving wilderness, think about the impact thousands and thousands of people like you can have who gain a similar environmental ethic and a sense of stewardship.

I fervently believe that taking a hike can be a catalyst for great personal change, eventually global change. Muir said it another way: "Between every two pine trees is a door to a new life." Find out for yourself the truth of his words. To be a wise caretaker of the environment doesn't mean you have to take on the entire planet. Just begin where you are, right now, today. Start in your backyard or find that last great place that is home to your soul, that special spot where the earth is alive and so are you.

Trail Etiquette and Safety

The use and enjoyment of wilderness requires special thoughtfulness and stewardship because beautiful backcountry areas serve a much greater purpose than playgrounds for day hikers and backpackers. John Muir once said that he wanted "to do something to make the mountains glad." Each of us can follow his lead when we visit the Eastern Sierra or any other natural area.

We all can "do something" by realizing that we are not entering a virtual reality. As ever-increasing numbers of people turn to wilderness for recreation and solitude, we should keep in mind that we are only temporary wayfarers passing through a real world of living things dependent on a healthy, intact ecosystem. We are but uninvited visitors in the home place of myriad species who can't survive anywhere else. This is their house. Be careful. Be considerate. Be respectful. Think about the impact, no matter how minute, your presence will have on the environment. Wilderness is fragile; tread softly on the landscape. The following suggestions should help you "make the mountains glad" while giving you a safe experience wandering Eastern Sierra canyons. Because hiking on trails inflicts the least damage on the landscape, all outings in this guide follow time-honored routes.

TRAIL MANNERS

Religiously avoid making new trails and shortcutting switchbacks. Following established trails minimizes the human footprint in wilderness. Limit group size on trails to fifteen people, eight for cross-country travel. Crowds and the accompanying noise greatly lessen the outdoor experience. Smaller is always better. During early season when trails are soft and wet, resist walking alongside the path to avoid squashing vegetation and creating ugly channels. If humanly possible, stay out of meadows, particularly if they are soggy. Instead, walk around them. If you must cross a trailless meadow and you're walking with companions, fan out so that numerous footsteps in tandem don't create a rut.

Hikers should always yield to equestrians, who have the right of way on trails. Move off trail and QUIETLY wait for the last horse or mule to pass. Courteous hikers will also step off trail for uphill trekkers. Dogs are permitted, but not encouraged, in national forest wilderness regions, and they are not allowed in designated bighorn sheep habitats or on trails in national parks. Dogs can and do harass and frighten wildlife and other hikers. Recommendation: leave Fido at home. Mountain bikes are not permitted in wilderness areas. Trailhead access roads, however, often provide excellent riding.

You may be surprised to know that you can live just fine for a day or two without electronic gadgets! Leave your city toys at home or locked in the car. Besides spectacular scenery, the absence of human generated noise is a huge—and often overlooked—component of wilderness. Don't diminish and trivialize such a glorious experience with cell phones, two-way radios, recorded music, hollering, nonstop loud conversations, etc. They ruin the ambiance for you and anyone near you and scare away wildlife. If detaching yourself from a cell phone for a few hours is going to send you into therapy, then use it ONLY in the event of a true (and unlikely) emergency.

Please do not deface, destroy or remove natural features, and leave historic artifacts in place. It's illegal and simply wrong to do so. Don't pick or trample wildflowers or other vegetation. Leave them alone to re-seed and for others to enjoy. Do your part and keep wilderness free of litter. Carry a trash bag and pick up any garbage left behind by careless, thoughtless hikers. Remember not to toss apple cores or orange and banana peels for animals to eat because 99 percent of the time they don't.

SANITATION

Make every effort to leave no trace of your visit. If you packed it in, you can pack it out. Human excrement is a big problem in the backcountry because it takes years to decompose, and when improperly disposed of, it can contaminate water quality. Find a spot at least 150 feet (60 paces) away from any water, trail or campsite, dig a cat hole 6 to 8 inches deep in organic soil, and cover thoroughly when done. NEVER bury toilet paper, tampons or diapers. Pack them out in a ziplock plastic bag because they can be dug up by animals and exposed by spring runoff. Nothing is more disgusting in wilderness than to see or smell the remains and trappings of human waste. Fish guts should also be buried deep and well away from water.

Never wash yourself or anything else in streams and lakes. All soaps, including those labeled biodegradable, change the chemical balance, ultimately polluting and harming all organisms that live in the water. Do your washing at least 100 feet (40 paces) away from the water. A tip: wet sand is excellent for washing dishes and hands.

SAFETY

One of the most important Golden Rules cautions us never to hike alone. This is especially good advice if you're a babe in the woods, so to speak. But if you do, then hit the trail overprepared for anything Mother Nature or your own inexperience might throw your way. Don't attempt cross-country travel unless you have map-reading and compass skills. The Sierra Nevada has a reputation for being a hospitable wilderness blessed with a temperate climate during summer. However, the mountains can be a dangerous world if common sense and good judgment do not accompany you on the trail.

Novice and veteran hikers alike need to be prepared for unexpected accidents and the whims of Sierra weather. A cloudless sunny morning can quickly deteriorate with the onset of a nasty rain or snowstorm. If you're new to mountain trail rambling, hike or backpack a number of times with an experienced friend or join a hiking club. There are also several helpful books on the market about the art of hiking.

One of the most exciting, appealing aspects of being out there in wilderness is the presence of unexpected risks and situations unknown to us in the city. Every hiker should be aware of and accept the possibility of unavoidable events. This book can't possibly list all the potential challenges and hazards you may encounter. The following suggestions, however, will provide basic and general information for your safety and enjoyment. At the very least, comply with all Forest Service regulations when visiting wilderness areas.

1. Always tell someone about your itinerary and ask them to contact the authorities if you don't call by an approximate prearranged time.

2. Know your limitations and physical capability, as well as current weather conditions. You are putting yourself in harm's way if you choose a hike beyond your fitness level, are not properly equipped, and/or ignore adverse weather. Example: A certain 12-mile-round-trip hike with an elevation gain of 3000 feet captures your fancy. But you have never walked farther than one flat mile, are wearing sandals, forgot water and snacks, and it looks like it might snow.

3. Be extremely careful with fire. Never smoke on the trail. With today's lightweight backpacking stoves and modern fabrics, there is really no need for a campfire. Besides, they are generally not permitted above 9600 feet. If you must have one, use an existing rock fire ring, keep it very small and burn only downed dead wood. Never remove limbs from a standing dead tree because they provide shelter for many creatures. Make sure your fire is completely out before moving on.

4. Don't hike at night.

5. Drink water often and before you're thirsty. Some Sierra water sources may contain giardia and cryptosporidium, which can cause miserable gastrointestinal symptoms. Day-trippers should be able to tote sufficient water for the hike. Backpackers should use a water filter or boil water for five minutes. Iodine, etc., is not effective treatment for waterborne cysts.

6. Eat before you're hungry. Carry a little extra food, too. Munch high-energy snacks—trail mix, power bars, jerky—rather than down a lunch fit for Godzilla. Hiking at high elevation, especially uphill, on a packed tummy is a recipe for nausea, cramps and general discomfort. Your body will always choose respiration over digestion.

7. A few gear items are important. You needn't be decked out like a walking advertisement for everything in an REI catalog, but there are some essentials for your comfort and safety. Some items overlap for day hikers and packers. Obviously, backpackers will need more and different equipment and food for multiple days in backcountry and should take everything they'll need—but not one ounce more. Every ounce counts when it's on your back. The following suggestions will serve you well on your hike.

◆ A hiking stick or hiking poles save knees and ankles and are helpful when crossing streams.

◆ Sunscreen, sunglasses, lip balm

◆ Mosquito repellent, especially in early season or near water

◆ First-aid kit

◆ Plastic whistle. Its sound carries farther than your voice in case you need help. SOS=three blasts.

◆ Appropriate clothing in case of temperature drop, wind, rain or snow. Never wear new untested boots or cotton socks. Layered clothing is advised. Always carry waterproof rain gear, no matter how warm or sunny it is at the trailhead.

◆ Map. Compass if you know how to use it

◆ All-purpose pocketknife

◆ Lightweight Mylar space blanket for emergency shelter, except in a lightning storm

◆ Any special medication you need

SPECIAL SAFETY PRECAUTIONS

STREAM CROSSINGS

Never underestimate the power of moving water, especially during peak snow melt. A surprising number of people have drowned while crossing Sierra streams. Bottom line, don't attempt a ford if the water is above your knees. Otherwise, try to cross early in the morning when the water level is at its lowest for the day. Unbuckle your pack's waist belt and loosen shoulder straps for a quick exit in case you fall. Do this even if you can cross on a log or rocks.

Unless you have extra footwear, remove your socks and only wear boots in the water. (Sandals or sneakers are good for crossing if you have dry boots to continue hiking with.) Soggy socks cause blisters. NEVER cross barefooted or tethered to a rope. Use a stout stick or two for balance, face upstream, and cross diagonally where the stream is wider and shallower. Be certain you are well above a cascade or stream confluence. If using just one stick for support, always plant it on the upstream side.

LIGHTNING

Lightning storms are common in the Sierra Nevada during summer. These lofty mountains are weather-makers. Sudden, sometimes violent, afternoon or early evening thunderstorms can pop up on any given day in High Country. Although these storms are usually short-lived, if you're caught in one, life can be very unpleasant—even dangerous—for a while. Hikers must be prepared and know what to do or else risk bodily harm, even death.

The wisest course of action is to don rain gear, abort the hike, and immediately boogie downhill if the sky darkens, thunderheads are building, and lightning dances nearby. Better yet, don't even start out if these conditions are in place at the trailhead. Understand that it's only going to get worse. Take responsibility for yourself and know when to call it quits.

Bear in mind that you do not want to be a lightning rod. If a storm threatens, the safest place to be is in a dense forest or at least a clump of trees. Should you get caught in an open area where you are the tallest thing around, remove your pack and get away from all metal objects. Absolutely do not huddle next to someone. Squat on your haunches, not on your butt, hug yourself and wait it out. The idea here is to keep your body parts off the ground. Lug soles on your boots could be your new best friend. If you have an insulated foam pad in your pack, sit on it. Never take shelter in rock caves or crevices, at the base of a cliff, near overhanging talus, under a lone tree, or near water.

HYPOTHERMIA

Hypothermia means below normal internal body temperature. It is a serious, albeit preventable, condition that kills more hikers than any other situation in the mountains. Even a drop of a few degrees can lead to physical and mental collapse and death if untreated. The classic ingredients for hypothermia include cold, wet, windy weather, exacerbated by exhaustion coupled with wet clothes and wind chill.

Take note that hypothermia more often than not happens in temperatures above freezing if the wet clothes and cold wind scenario is in place. The body loses heat more rapidly in combination with those factors. The symptoms are: uncontrolled shivering, slurred speech, poor motor coordination, sleepiness, impaired thinking, and eventually coma. Unfortunately, very often the stricken person is in stubborn denial that he/she is in grave danger. This is another reason hiking alone is not a good idea.

Prevention is the key. Take action BEFORE you're soaking wet. First and foremost, keep your clothes dry by having waterproof, not water repellent, rain gear in your pack—always. Hikers and backpackers should faithfully wear or carry ample insulated clothing. Wool and synthetic fabrics, such as polypropylene and pile, will insulate even when wet. Cotton and down materials are to be avoided as protection against hypothermia.

Someone with symptoms must be warmed immediately. At the first sign of shivering, get yourself or another out of the weather and wet clothes ASAP. Especially if hiking solo, waste no time getting down the mountain and into dry clothes. If backpacking alone, get in the tent, strip, and snuggle in your sleeping bag. If you're with someone, the best way to warm up is to have skin-to-skin contact within a sleeping bag. Drinking hot liquids and eating high-energy food usually hasten recovery and are more effective than a fire.

ALTITUDE SICKNESS

Most flatlanders will feel the effects of hiking, even strolling, in high elevation. The brain does funny things when deprived of the oxygen it is accustomed to. Keep in mind that there is one-third less oxygen at 10,000 feet than there is at sea level. Because it may take a few days to acclimate, the ideal solution to minimize altitude sickness is to spend two or three days at altitude before hitting the trail.

If that is not possible, then hike slowly and for a shorter distance, rest often, eat quick energy food (candy, dried fruit, energy bars), and drink LOTS of water. Give your body a chance to adjust to a much more demanding environment than it's used to.

Decreased oxygen levels cause some people to experience headache, nausea, shortness of breath, fast pulse, crankiness, and appetite loss. Most symptoms are mild and not life threatening. However, if symptoms worsen—bloody sputum, vomiting, severe shortness of breath and extreme exhaustion—flee to a lower elevation immediately and seek medical help. These are very serious conditions. Know that altitude sickness can strike some people at 4000 or 5000 feet, relatively low elevations, and it has nothing to do with age or fitness.

BEARS

All bears in the Sierra Nevada are American black bears, though they may be brown, cinnamon or even blonde. They are intelligent, shy, excellent climbers, swift runners, relatively unaggressive and always hungry. Their appetite is the primary source of concern to the majority of Sierra visitors. It's very unlikely you'll see one on the trail. Consider yourself a blessed hiker if you do witness one of these magnificent critters. Should it happen, stay out of its space, give it room to escape, don't provoke it, don't try to feed it, and especially do not come between a mother and her cubs. I've seen a few bruins over the years in my wilderness rambles, but I have never felt threatened by them.

Undoubtedly, you've heard about the so-called bear problem in the Sierra, especially in and around Yosemite and Sequoia-Kings Canyon National Parks. More accurately, however, it's definitely a people problem. The majority of encounters occur in campgrounds and popular backpackers' camps. Long ago bears learned to associate humans with easy food sources. Careless campers and former ineffective wildlife management practices in national parks and forests have created scavenger bears addicted to human food. Food and other scented items left in accessible garbage bins, tents, coolers, picnic tables, and vehicles are open invitations to a bear. You can't fault a bear for preferring a big bag of Oreos to a mouthful of manzanita berries!

It is now your legal responsibility to keep food from bears in national parks and forests. If a bear gets away with your improperly stored groceries, it is your problem, and you can be fined. Don't expect any sympathy from the authorities. Remember: A fed bear is a dead bear. Many bears are euthanized each year because of their dependence on human food.

MOUNTAIN LIONS

You have a far better chance of spotting a fleet of UFOs in the Sierra than a mountain lion. Even lifelong hikers such as myself have never seen one of these great cats. By nature, they are nocturnal, reclusive, and have an important place in the food chain. Unfortunately, a few much publicized accounts of cougar attacks have inordinately frightened the public and raised a hue and cry for their extermination. Know that the threat of an attack is exaggerated.

In the highly unlikely event you do see one, give our largest predator the respect it deserves. Although it will go against your instincts and take a heap of will power, DO NOT turn and run from it. If it doesn't scamper away, make yourself appear large and powerful, look at it, shout and wave your arms as if you were ready and able to defend yourself. Mountain lions are more apt to attack an animal that runs away from them than one that remains immobile. In truth, you should be more concerned about protecting yourself from biting flies and gazillions of bloodthirsty mosquitoes that pester hikers in early season and around water sources.

WHERE AM I?

If you follow the guidelines in this book you'll be hiking on established trails and needn't fret about getting lost. Nonetheless, pay attention to your surroundings. If you're hiking with companions and come to a trail junction, marked or unmarked, always wait there until everyone catches up. Should you step off trail for a photo, to relieve yourself, etc., leave your pack at that point. In case you become confused and lose the trail, your pack will identify the spot for someone to start looking. Don't panic and start wandering around. Stay put and wait for help to come to you. Give three blasts on your whistle and repeat until you're located.

BACKCOUNTRY CAMPING

Because they stay longer than day hikers, backpackers have a greater potential for negatively impacting the landscape. On the other hand, as John Muir suggested, they have an opportunity to make the mountains glad. More than a million people camp in Sierra wilderness annually. High Country is, literally, being loved to death, and we all have to work together to protect it. If we don't, the wilderness values we go there to enjoy will either seriously degrade, as they have in many places, or disappear entirely. We can become responsible stewards by learning how to limit our impact. It's really not that difficult to do.

Follow these tips to safeguard fragile irreplaceable wilderness areas. Modern equipment, enlightened techniques and a heightened environmental consciousness give us the ability to walk softly on the land and Leave No Trace of our visit. Pick a site at least 60 paces away from water and the trail. Choose an existing site, and don't modify it in any way, such as trenching around tents, leveling the ground, building new fire rings, or damaging trees and vegetation.

If you must camp on a new site, pick a hard or durable spot, such as sand, gravel, hard ground or rock slabs. NEVER make camp in meadows or atop any kind of vegetation. At high elevation, it takes many decades to heal damaged vegetation and compacted or eroded soil. Just remember that everything up there is necessary for the survival of some animal or plant.

CAMPFIRES.

Campfires are obsolete. There is simply not enough wood at high elevation to waste on a fire, which is essentially unnecessary in the first place. Spare the trees and use an efficient, lightweight backpacker's stove. Dead or alive, trees are not only an integral and aesthetically valuable part of the scenery, but they also provide food and shelter for a host of species. They're also critical as decomposed organic material needed to enrich thin High Country soil. Moreover, campfires are not permitted above 9600 feet, and in some locations, the limit is 9000 feet. Even at lower elevations, fires are discouraged.

There are many excellent reasons not to build a fire. Among them, you and your gear won't smell like smoke; you'll have a much wider choice of campsites; the chance of bear coming to see what's on the menu is greatly reduced; stoves work even if it's raining or snowing; you can gaze at starlight instead of firelight.

If you choose to ignore current wisdom and sound environmental principles, try to camp where there is already a rock fire ring. Don't build a new one. Keep it really small, and use only dead wood that's on the ground. Never leave it unattended. Before you break camp, make sure it is out and cold to the touch. Remember always to pack out anything that didn't burn.

Wilderness is THE authority. Your actions can protect the qualities you came searching for. Set an example that others can follow for centuries.

~ Stuart Weiss

The Climate

Because of its colossal length and great height, the Sierra Nevada range exhibits a wide diversity of weather patterns. Temperatures and precipitation vary significantly between foothill and summit areas. In the subalpine and alpine regions (8500 feet to 14,000 feet plus) of High Country, the mountains are notorious weather-makers. Relative to elevation and which side of the Sierra you're considering, there are several climate zones. The Eastern Sierra is much more arid because moisture-laden clouds drop most of their water as they ascend the long western slope. By the time wet air masses reach the crest and arrive on the east side, most of the moisture has been squeezed out.

Of considerable concern to hikers during summer is the appearance of subtropical storms up from northern Mexico and the Gulf of California. As they move through the Great Basin from southwest to northeast, they carry wet, unstable air which can blanket the entire range with rain, hail or snow depending on elevation. These moisture-rich events, as a rule, last longer than the more typical afternoon thunderstorms.

The disparate climates of the hot and dry high desert and the arctic zone near the crest are separated by only a few miles. In June, for example, at the foot of the Eastern Sierra wall in Bishop, spring is already a pleasant memory, and summer is in full swing. Yet, just a short distance away and 7000 feet above at Pine Creek Pass, winter still has an icy grip on the landscape. This striking, unique closeness of desert and alpine climates is certainly one of the alluring features that draws visitors to the Eastern Sierra.

Eastern Sierra climate is quite good-natured compared to other vast mountain ranges worldwide. However, High Country hoofers should never take a sunny, wind-calm morning at the trailhead for granted. Although generally benign in summer and early fall, mountain weather can degrade quickly. An afternoon thunderstorm is a force to be reckoned with as many hikers have learned. Amidst bellicose thunder claps, wild slithers of lightning, fierce, swirling winds, heavy rain, hail and sometimes snow, unprepared sojourners will be miserable during these occasional bad-tempered fits. Moreover, getting smacked by lightning is a real danger in the High Sierra.

If caught in one of these usually brief tempests, even if you are properly prepared, you may heartily disagree with a wag who believes "there is no such thing as bad weather, only different kinds of good weather." Every hiker needs to carry warm clothing and waterproof rain gear—ALWAYS—and know what to do on the trail when a thunderstorm strikes (See Special Safety Precautions on page 19).

Take note that the winter snow pack can have a big impact on your summer hiking plans. In heavy snowfall years, many high trails may not be clear until mid-August. If snowfall is light, the same trails may be clear by early July. Be advised that spring runoff after a heavy winter equals hazardous and/or impossible stream crossings, often until midsummer.

Take responsibility for your safety, and be prepared before you hit the trail! Get as much weather and trail information as possible prior to your visit to the Eastern Sierra. Contact local visitor centers, Forest Service ranger stations or National Park Service information for current weather and trail conditions. Above all, stay flexible and use common sense. Change your hiking destination, abort it en route or postpone it if conditions are dangerous and the weather is threatening.

The Geology

Born in volcanic fury millions of years ago, the 430-mile-long by 50-to-80-mile-wide Sierra Nevada range stretches between Tehachapi Pass and the Cascades north of the Feather River. It occupies a huge portion of California and a wee corner of Nevada around Lake Tahoe. It's also the longest, most continuous mountain range in the lower 48 states. From sun-baked foothill lowlands to the cool alpine reaches of 14,000-foot peaks, the Sierra Nevada is a region of phenomenal beauty and staggering biodiversity.

The violent uplift of a titanic body of granite created a short, very steep eastern escarpment and a long, gradual western slope tilted toward the Pacific Ocean. Since its cataclysmic birth, the forces of nature continue to shape the topography. The actions of wind, weather and water are constantly fine-tuning the mountains. Before the earth cooled and glaciers formed, erosive processes attacked the young range, plucking rock from mountainsides and washing it down rivers into a shallow sea that extended across present-day Nevada. Later, between about one million and 10,000 years ago, great tongues of ice quarried and sculpted bedrock into exquisite geological formations. More than any other natural force, at least six ice ages defined the Sierra's stunning, unique landscape.

The Eastern Sierra Nevada is a vast land of extreme contrasts and dramatic scenery. Fascinated by its tempestuous volcanic origin and stark splendor, John Muir described it as "Hot deserts bounded by snow-laden mountains, cinders and ashes scattered on glacial polished pavements, frost and fire working together in the making of beauty."

Born in volcanic fire and chiseled by glacial ice, the Eastern Sierra is a powerful, extraordinary bioregion containing quintessential scenery and countless recreational opportunities. In contrast to its western counterpart blessed with more rain, large rivers and dense forests and vegetation, the Eastern Sierra captures little moisture, has few and scattered forests with scanty undergrowth and small streams. But the sparseness of vegetation allows the eye endless and unrestricted horizons. Truly, on a clear day you can see forever.

The region's numerous water- and glacier-carved canyons that deeply gash the eastern ramparts are superb arenas for immersing yourself in its astounding collage of scenery, geology, flora, fauna and human history. Donald Peattie offers a vivid snapshot of this rugged, enchanting land in *A Natural History of Western Trees*. "The eastern face of this range . . . forms, in places, one of the steepest, swiftest descents—almost a downward plunge of the planet's surface. It faces the desert, and its slopes are arid. At first this side of the Sierra appears much less hospitable and charming, and it is certainly less accessible. But in time one comes to have a special affection for its dramatic scenery, for its pure, cold lakes so secretively concealed, for the bracing dryness of its air, for its greater wildness and lack of milling throngs of our fellow humans."

Although this book's purpose is to guide visitors into twenty-five of the many eastside canyons, the Eastern Sierra technically encompasses a much larger territory. In fact, it is the convergence of the Sierra Nevada, Great Basin, White Mountains and Mojave Desert. Technically, a definition must include its entire 430-mile length, including the vast high desert terrain east of the base of the massive, snow-spangled mountain wall. However, it is the 125-mile span of High Country south of Sonora Pass that is commonly considered to be the heart and soul of the Eastern Sierra.

Travelers should not shun the Spartan high desert environment that abuts the towering Sierra eastern escarpment. It, too, is a region of great, though subtle, scenic value. The desert exhibits a quiet beauty and a peaceful, laid-back charisma very different from the high drama of its neighboring granite ramparts. Every species that lives in this parched landscape is weather-toughened and well adapted to rainfall measured by the tablespoon. At first glance and from a distance, it may seem like a bleak, sandy world populated only by sagebrush and lizards. However, forests of Jeffrey pine, piñon pine and aspen can be found on the mountain slopes and in canyons. In early season, flowers blanket this seemingly desolate land. In wet years, such as 2004-2005, the usually monochromatic landscape transforms to a wildly colorful sea of wildflowers. Numerous, lonely byways ply this land of little rain, leading to ghost towns, tiny settlements, hardscrabble ranches, historic mining camps and strangely beautiful scenery. The desert is full of life, but you have to look for it. In time, this minimalist setting will grow on you and lure you back to probe its secret places.

The real voyage of discovery consists not in seeking new landscapes, but in having new eyes. ~ Marcel Proust

Human History of the Eastern Sierra

Humans have lived in the Eastern Sierra for a very long time. The beautiful mountain-desert world you love to visit was inhabited by semi-nomadic Mono and Paiute Indians for thousands of years before "discovery" by European-Americans. They, too, surely appreciated its wondrous scenery as well as a variety of seasonally available food sources needed to sustain life. Because the indigenous people had a negligible impact on the land, very little remains for us to know about their culture prior to contact, even less about prehistoric cultures.

Regrettably, early written accounts of Eastern Sierra native people are terse and biased. Subsequent descriptions, which increase in number as settlers arrived in the mid-1800s, are written from the skewed viewpoint of those who sought justification for killing and evicting Indians from their ancestral homeland. During the 1920s, anthropologists attempted to study and record traditional land use and lifestyle, but it was too little, too late. This tragic loss of knowledge of an ancient people is summed up by archaeologist Robert Bettinger, ". . . by the time the pathetic battles had all been fought, diseases had run their course, major villages had been abandoned, native life ways existed only in the memories of the few aged individuals born long before the first white settlement was first built . . ."

We do know, however, that several passes provided travel and trade corridors between eastern and western tribes. Artifacts have been found throughout the range, even atop alpine peaks and in remote canyons. Mono Pass, for example, on present-day Yosemite's eastern edge, was an important Indian trade route for 9600 years before the obliteration of their culture by European-Americans in the mid-nineteenth century. Hikers may chance upon obsidian fragments, broken projectile points, mortar cups, rock (house) rings and petroglyphs, or mysterious designs, pecked on boulders. Please don't remove them or disturb these irreplaceable reminders of a bygone people. The artifacts belong where you found them and have much more value connected with the landscape.

The Paiute and Mono peoples of historic times were preceded by other native people who were in the region for thousands of years before those encountered by early explorers. Projectile points more than 10,000 years old bear witness to the existence of prehistoric groups. Next to nothing is known about this vastly older culture. Even modern-day Indians profess no knowledge of the ancient ones.

The early explorers, so-called mountain men, and initial prospectors had little effect on native Eastern Sierra people. However, before long, the lure of gold and silver in the mid-1800s marked the beginning of the end for the native's traditional lifestyle. There never were large populations of Monos and Paiutes, and the influx of miners and settlers rapidly pushed them to the brink of extinction. They were displaced from prime camping and food gathering locations close to water, which were also the most desirable lands for farming and ranching. The Indians were forced to occupy marginal land on which they could no longer effectively hunt and gather food.

Vast numbers of cattle and sheep herded into Eastern Sierra valleys and meadows devastated native food sources. Piñon and Jeffrey pines were felled by the thousands for mine timbers, fuel and lumber. The clear-cutting of piñons was especially detrimental because pine nuts were an extremely important nutritious food staple. Livestock overgrazed and trampled grasslands that provided precious food resources, such as tubers, roots and seeds. Furthermore, persistent hunting by the settlers virtually wiped out populations of game and waterfowl.

Early Basque sheepherders created arborglyphs like this on the smooth bark of resident aspen trees, some of which can still be found today.

Faced with starvation and suffering from violence and bloodshed, by 1870 the local native peoples had little choice but to work on ranches and farms when they could no longer hunt and gather food on their ancestral lands. The subjugation and irrevocable alteration of their culture was a shameful chapter in Eastern Sierra history, as it was everywhere else in North America. Still, there are bright spots. Recently, an increasing interest and appreciation for Mono and Paiute culture have spurred the development of interpretive displays, exhibits and cultural centers that portray their traditional lifestyle. Despite the dismantling of most of their ancestral range and way of life in the nineteenth century, modern Monos and Paiutes have been able to survive and remain in the Eastern Sierra.

The proliferation of ranching, farming and lumbering was sparked by the region's silver and gold mining activity. Even after the boom years, agriculture continued to flourish. By the early years of the twentieth century, a few rustic resorts were forerunners of the huge tourist industry looming on the horizon.

At the same time, Los Angeles officials came to the Eastern Sierra in hot pursuit of tapping into the area's abundant, high-quality water to meet the needs of a rapidly growing community. A prolonged, knockdown water war ensued between the locals and Los Angeles that to a degree is still being fought. An excellent book that discusses the bitter battle in detail is *Deepest Valley*, by Genny Smith.

Thanks to all-year roads into the region, recreation and tourism burgeoned, nudging out agriculture as the primary economic force. It began in 1915 with the opening of a trans-Sierra road over Tioga Pass, allowing access to the east side. Although built in segments, a paved highway between Los Angeles and Bridgeport was completed between 1916 and 1931. In time it became Highway 395, the Eastern Sierra's immensely scenic corridor along the base of the mountains. An influx of Hollywood luminaries, among the initial tourists to vacation in the area, contributed to the development of resorts, vacation homes and other facilities to accommodate them.

"Build it and they will come" seemed an appropriate and often repeated mantra of the era. In truth, in places like Mammoth, large-scale development is a fact of life. Today, as always, the Eastern Sierra has a well-deserved reputation as a region of outstanding scenic, historic and recreational resources. Fortunately, there are organizations dedicated to preserving the sublime scenery and prodigious biodiversity. These groups also fully understand that healthy, intact ecosystems benefit everyone and everything on the landscape.

Rustic Resorts of the Eastern Sierra

Doc and Al's Resort 760-932-7051, Box 266, Bridgeport, CA 93517, elevation 7000 feet, established 1957, has 23 pine-shaded rustic cabins and grassy campsites along Robinson Creek in Toiyabe National Forest. Fully furnished housekeeping cabins with picnic tables and barbecues. Trout fishing at your doorstep or in numerous nearby lakes and streams. Reasonable rates. No TV, 2 pay phones, fee for pets, laundry, ice, fishing tackle. Located on Twin Lakes Road southwest of Bridgeport.

Twin Lakes Resort 760-932-7751, Box 248, Bridgeport, CA 93517, elevation 7200 feet, 8 housekeeping cottages southwest of Bridgeport on Twin Lakes Road. Fee for pets, laundromat, general store, fishing tackle, trailer park, boat rentals. Café nearby.

Hunewill Guest Ranch 760-932-7710 in summer, 760-465-2201 in winter, Box 368, Bridgeport, CA 93517 or www.hunewillranch.com, elevation 6500 feet, established 1861. Working cattle ranch is family owned and operated. Located southwest of Bridgeport off Twin Lakes Road in an enormous meadow. Equestrian oriented lodging at pricey dude ranch on 4500 acres. Comfortable cottages, includes all meals in the founder's Victorian ranch house. Offers various packages, activities. No pets, child care and massage therapist available. Pay phone, laundry and gift shop.

Virginia Lakes Resort 760-647-6484, HCR62, Box 1065, Bridgeport, CA 93517 or www.virginialakesresort.com, elevation 9770 feet, established 1923. Several rustic cabins located in a beautiful, colorful setting adjacent to Virginia Lakes and trailhead into lake-filled Virginia Canyon destinations. Small store, good café for breakfast and lunch. Tackle/fishing licenses, no motorized boats or swimming allowed in Big and Little Virginia Lakes. Rowboat rentals, fee for pets.

Virginia Creek Settlement 760-932-7780, HCR50, Box 1050, Bridgeport, CA 93517 or www.virginiacrksettlement.com, elevation 6700 feet. Comfortable creekside rooms and log cabins. Closest lodging near Bodie State Historic Park. Small restaurant serves excellent breakfast and dinner.

Lundy Lake Resort 626-309-0415, Box 550, Lee Vining, CA 93541, elevation 7800 feet. Basic housekeeping cabins, small general store and campground with piped water at the head of Lundy Lake beneath towering peaks. Shared public baths. Boat rentals, dogs OK.

Tioga Pass Resort 254-241-6259, Box 7, Lee Vining, CA 93541, or www.tiogapassresort.com, email: reservations@tiogapassresort.com, elevation 9600 feet. Located along Tioga Pass Road 9 miles west of Highway 395 and Lee Vining. Housekeeping cabins and sleep-only units next to Lee Vining Creek. Very good breakfast, lunch and dinner in small café. Colorful High Sierra setting just east of Tioga Pass. Small store. No pets.

Saddlebag Lake Resort (no phone), PO Box 303, Lee Vining, CA 93541, or www.saddlebaglakeresort.com, email: staff@saddlebaglakeresortcom, elevation 10,100 feet. Rustic cabins above the lake, the highest drive-to lake in California. Good café and small store in Inyo National Forest just east of Tioga Pass, 11 miles northwest of Lee Vining. Campground nearby. Dramatic High Country setting. First cabin was built in early 1900s for use as a trapper's shelter. Original cabin has been upgraded by successive owners. Boat "taxi" available for a fee to reach highly scenic Twenty Lakes Basin beyond the north end of the lake.

Silver Lake Resort 760-648-7525, Box 116, June Lake, CA 93529 or www.silverlakeresort.net, elevation 7240 feet, established 1916. Touted as the "oldest resort in the Eastern Sierra." Rustic and more modern housekeeping cabins on the north shore of lovely Silver Lake on the June Lake Loop Road. Country store and excellent homestyle café food for breakfast and dinner. Boat and canoe rentals. RV park next to Rush Creek. Pets OK on leash.

Fern Creek Lodge 800-621-9146, Route 3, Box 7, June Lake, CA 93529 or www.ferncreeklodge.com, elevation 7600 feet, established 1927. "June Lake Loop's oldest year-round resort." Housekeeping cabins between Gull and Silver Lakes. Store, sporting goods. Fee for pets. Group, weekly and ski package specials.

Convict Lake Resort 800-992-2260, Route 1, Box 204, Mammoth Lakes, CA 93546 or www.convictlake.com, elevation 7600 feet. Near Convict Lake 2 miles west of Highway 395, 9 miles south of Mammoth. Outstanding restaurant open nightly year-round. Housekeeping cabins, general store, canoe rentals, guided horseback rides. Showers for hikers for a fee. Fee for pets. Heavenly setting surrounded by colorful peaks.

Tom's Place 760-935-4239, HCR79, Crowley Lake, CA 93546 or www.tomsplaceresort.com, elevation 7000 feet, eastablished 1917. Located at junction of Crowley Lake Drive and Rock Creek Road just off Highway 395, 14 miles south of Mammoth. Rustic lodge rooms and housekeeping cabins. General store, post office, café and bar. Pets allowed in three cabins. Reasonable rates.

Rock Creek Lakes Resort 760-935-4311, Box 727, Bishop, CA 93515 or www.rockcreeklake.com, elevation 9700 feet, established 1923. 1-3 bedroom rustic and newer cabins. Located on Rock Creek Road 9 miles west of Tom's Place in Rock Creek Canyon, one of the most stunning settings in the entire Eastern Sierra. Excellent food in small café, also serving the best homemade pies in the Eastern Sierra. General store and boat rentals. Showers for hikers for a fee. No pets.

Eastern Sierra Pack Stations North of Bishop

Discover the Sierra from a saddle the way your ancestors did. The spectacular canyons of the Eastern Sierra are a great place for horse powered trips with professional pack outfits. Trips may be arranged in a wide variety of ways. Spot trips, trail rides, all-inclusive trips, hiking with pack stock, extended wilderness base camps and backpacker food drops to name a few. For a brochure describing horse packing adventures, contact the Eastern Sierra Packers Association at the Bishop Visitor Center 888-395-3952 or www.bishopvisitor.com.

"There is something about the outside of a horse that is good for the inside of a man." See for yourself if Winston Churchill's advice rings true.

Leavitt Meadows Pack Outfit: email bartat@leavittmeadows.com or www.leavittmeadows.com. They invite you to "see the Sierra from a saddle." They're located on Sonora Pass Road (Highway 108) 7 miles west of Highway 395. Established in the early 1930s, Leavitt Meadows Pack Outfit offers a full menu of trips from day rides to full-service backcountry base camps to fly fishing excursions. They service the territory in the West Walker River drainage in the proposed addition to Hoover Wilderness.

Virginia Lakes Pack Outfit 760-937-0326 in summer, 707-459-2485 in winter, or www.virginialakes.com. Find them 12 miles south of Bridgeport and 5 miles west of Highway 395 on Virginia Lakes Road. They provide various trips in Hoover Wilderness, northern Yosemite, featuring custom "gourmet camping for groups of 8." This outfit believes their trips will show you a part of Yosemite wilderness few people will ever see.

Frontier Pack Train 760-648-7701 in summer, 760-873-7971 in winter, or www.frontierpacktrain.com. Near Silver Lake on June Lake Loop Road. Their outfit accommodates anglers, photographers and others for backcountry access to thirty-five lakes in Ansel Adams Wilderness, plus wild mustang and horse drives.

Mammoth Lakes Pack Outfit 888-475-8747 in winter, or www.mammothpackoutfit.com. Established in 1915, it is Mammoth's oldest business. They service McGee and Baldwin Lakes, Hilton Canyon, Fish Creek and Convict Lake Basin. Many trip options are available, such as horse drives, daily and extended trips, backpacker assists, spot trips and extended backcountry camps.

Red's Meadow Pack Station and Agnew Meadow Pack Station (near Devils Postpile National Monument) 800-292-7758, or www.reds-meadow.com. Bob Tanner's two pack outfits do a great job of giving city slicker horse drives, day rides and multi-day pack trips. Hop on board one of his 120 horses for a memorable Eastern Sierra adventure. Area serviced is Devils Postpile, John Muir Wilderness and Ansel Adams Wilderness, Mount Whitney, plus Shadow, Ediza, Garnet and Thousand Island Lakes (beneath the stunning Minarets).

McGee Creek Pack Station 760-935-4324 in summer, 760-878-2207 in winter, or www.mcgeecreekpackstation.com. The Roesers offer individually tailored trips with many unique services available to suit every wilderness travel budget. All kinds of trips to remote, secluded areas in John Muir Wilderness. Easy access to the pack station at the end of McGee Creek Road, 7 miles north of Tom's Place.

Rock Creek Pack Station 760-872-8331 in winter, 760-935-4493 in summer, or www.rockcreekpackstation.com. Fully outfitted pack trips, spot trips, educational programs, hiking with pack stock and horse drives. Easiest access to Hilton Lakes, Little Lakes Valley, Pioneer and Hopkins Basins, Mono Creek and The Recesses. Find them at the end of Rock Creek Road, 10 miles west of Tom's Place.

Pine Creek Pack Station 800-962-0775, 760-387-2627, or www.395.com/berners. Established 1934, the corral and office can be found at the end of Pine Creek (canyon) Road, 19 miles northwest of Bishop and 39 miles south of Mammoth. All types of fully outfitted wilderness trips and hiker assists to Horton and Royce Lakes, streams and lakes of Pine Creek Canyon, French Canyon, Lake Italy, Granite Park, John Muir Wilderness and Kings Canyon National Park.

Useful Eastern Sierra Contacts

CalTrans Road Report: 1-800-427-ROAD

Mono County Sheriff: 760-932-7549

Bridgeport Chamber of Commerce: 760-932-7500

Toiyabe National Forest, Bridgeport Ranger District: 760-932-7070

Mono Basin Scenic Area Visitor Center/Lee Vining Ranger District: 760-647-3044

Mono Lake Committee Information Center/Bookstore/Canoe Tours/Lee Vining Chamber of Commerce: 760-647-6595

Mono Lake (eco) Boat Tours at Tioga Lodge: 1-888-647-6423

Yosemite National Park: 209-372-0200

June Lakes Chamber of Commerce: 760-648-7584

Mammoth Lakes Visitor Center and Ranger Station: 760-924-5500

Inyo County Sheriff & Search and Rescue: 760-878-0383

Mammoth Hospital: 760-934-3111

Inyo National Forest, White Mountain Ranger District: 760-873-2500

Adventures in Camping. vacation trailer rentals (They set up where you want it): 1-800-417-7771

The author between a rock and a hard place

Burt Canyon
Easy Rambling in the Hoover Wilderness

◆ THE DETAILS

Getting There: On Highway 395 drive 16 miles north of Bridgeport or 0.7 mile south of the 395/108 (Sonora Pass Road) intersection. Turn west on unpaved Little Walker River Road, signed "Little Walker River Road" from the south, "National Forest Campground" from the north. Drive 3.4 miles to a junction at Obsidian Campground. Bear right and drive 0.15 mile. Where the road forks bear left and drive uphill for one mile on a road cut into the slope. Parking is limited; do not block gate. The "official" signed parking area for Burt Canyon is next to the river just downhill from where you turned uphill. (The right fork continues 3.5 miles to Emma Lake Trailhead.)

Nearest Campground: Obsidian Campground, located along Molybdenite Creek, has 14 shaded fee sites for tents and small RVs. No piped water, non-reservable, tables, fire rings, pit toilets. Open May through October. Dogs OK on leash.

Lodging/Services: Walker, 14 miles north on Highway 395, has Andruss Motel 530-495-2166. In Bridgeport, a full service town 16 miles south, try Silver Maple Inn 760-932-7383. Hays Street Café serves excellent breakfast and lunch.

Further Info: Toiyabe National Forest, Bridgeport Ranger District 760-932-7070.

User Groups: Hikers and horses. Dogs OK on leash. No mountain bikes.

Hike Distance: 13.5 miles round trip to Anna Lake, 16 miles round trip to trail's end.

Difficulty: Variable, depending on your destination. Strenuous round trip to Anna Lake.

Elevation: 7800 feet at trailhead, 10,500 feet at Anna Lake.

Cautions: Watch for bears.

Best Times to Go: Early summer to late fall.

Other Maps: **Hoover Wilderness Map** or Tom Harrison's **Hoover Wilderness Trail Map** are the best. USGS Fales Hot Springs 7.5-minute topo.

Winter Sports: Road may be open and passable in winter, providing opportunities for cross-country skiing and snowshoeing.

OF INTEREST

◆ Very near Molybdenite Creek and Emma Lake trailheads.

◆ Close to highly scenic Sonora Pass for more hiking and outdoor recreation.

◆ Beautiful creekside and meadow wildflowers in early season.

◆ Brilliant fall foliage display.

◆ Fishing in Little Walker River.
◆ Lightly used trail.

Fortunately, for Eastern Sierra canyon fans who prefer less formidable hikes than can be found in most of these yawning chasms, a scattering of easier corridors reach into the backcountry. Among the lightly used trails is the Burt Canyon Trail northwest of Bridgeport, offering striking scenery and plentiful solitude. A check of the topo map reveals the contour intervals don't resemble a fingerprint, thus validating the trail's overall modest gradient.

Never far from Little Walker River, the route travels through a variety of vegetation zones in Toiyabe National Forest. Most of the 6.75-mile-long path to alpine Anna Lake lies within Hoover Wilderness. Although the round trip

mileage is rather long, the elevation gain is painless except for the steep pitch to the lake. Half of the rise in elevation occurs in the 1.25-mile grunt to its austere setting at 10,500 feet. Rest assured that there are no trail cops tracking how far or how fast you've walked. Proceed only as far as energy and time dictate.

Day hikers and backpackers will delight in the diverse charms of this secluded Sierra retreat in Toiyabe-Humboldt National Forest. At 4.3 million acres, most of which are in

The author's dog Cosie enjoys the shade of an immense Sierra juniper in Burt Canyon.

Along the trail in Burt Canyon

Nevada, it's the largest national forest in the lower 48 states. Widely diverse habitats and ecosystems exist within the sprawling territory. Because the topography is so variable, one can stand on a cool, pine-studded slope at 10,000 feet or higher and gaze down at an arid, sun-baked landscape covered with sage-shrub lands, juniper and piñon pines. You'll experience this contrast on your journey to Anna Lake.

Gigantic Sierra junipers and Jeffrey pines line the mile-long dirt road leading to a small parking area. Past the locked gate the unsigned trail starts out as an access road and dips gently into the canyon proper. The expansive view ahead is very eye-pleasing and beckons the visitor to walk into the heart of its beauty. For the next mile you are on Hanging Valley private property and will see a few antique trailers used occasionally in summer and fall.

The road skirts the edge of stream-cut Willow Flat at the entrance of a lush riparian habitat for wildflowers and wildlife. Hanging Valley is a geologic term referring to a tributary glacial valley whose mouth is above the main valley floor. At the end of private property, the road becomes a footpath. Burt Canyon is a must-see location for late spring and early summer wildflowers. Shrieks of color vie for your attention along the way. Rein orchid, iris, golden rod, green gentian, potentilla, Indian paintbrush, lupine and penstemon are among a passel of species in this flowery paradise.

Almost flat, the trail meanders through open, pungent sagebrush fields, stands of conifers, aspen groves and then into gorgeous high elevation meadows.

Snow-capped peaks above Burt Canyon

Arborglyphs, writing or designs carved by Basque shepherds, on some aspens testify that flocks of sheep once grazed in the grassy environment. The trail enters Hoover Wilderness around 2 miles.

Established in 1964, 48,601-acre Hoover Wilderness and its proposed 64,000-acre addition provide a broad range of hiking and other recreational options. Between 8,000 and 12,000 feet, magnificent scenery and primeval backcountry are tucked in among vast forests, meadows, glacier-carved canyons, icy streams, scores of lakes and wind-blasted granite peaks. A variety of trails and cross-country routes exist to capture your interest and lure you into pristine terrain. Backpackers can move between the Hoover Wilderness and neighboring Yosemite National Park via several passes.

The gently ascending trail crosses Little Walker River at 3.5 miles (1.5 miles inside the wilderness boundary). Plan on a wet ford in early season. Little Walker is not a deep, raging torrent, but exercise caution and common sense in crossing it. The stream will be on your left from here on. Walker Mountain, elevation 11,563 feet, is the prominent landmark in the foreground to the south. In another mile the path begins to curve southward and crosses a seasonal stringer flowing down Piute Canyon.

To the southwest, the crests (from right to left) of Flatiron Butte, Hanna Mountain and Ink Rocks define the southern limit of the Little Walker River drainage. Experienced peak baggers will be interested in a nontechnical climb to one or more of them. Some of the snow melt from these peaks will flow north and east to Walker Lake, a sink in Nevada near Hawthorne. The trail meets Anna Lake junction on the right 1.75 miles past Piute Canyon's creek and 5.5 miles from the trailhead.

Anna Lake, elevation 10,500 feet, is the primary destination for hikers who travel in Burt Canyon. The spur trail to the lake breaks away from the main trail on the right and climbs sharply. The abrupt, switchbacking route gains

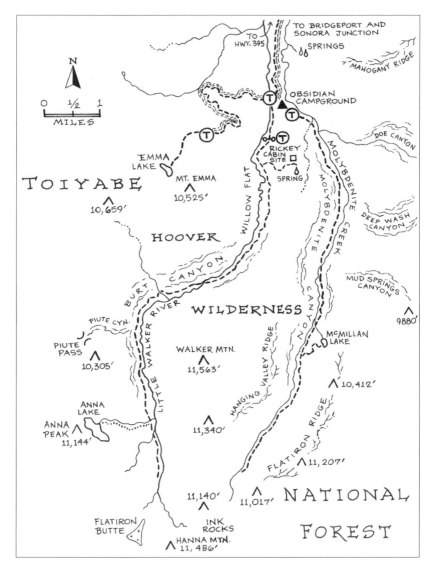

1300 feet in 1.25 miles. You'll likely encounter snow on the trail and a frozen or slushy lake until July in a year of normal precipitation. Anna Lake was probably named for Anna Mack who lived at Hardy Station near the intersection of Highways 395 and 108. Home to golden trout, the lake is surrounded by steep, unstable scree—rocky rubble—slopes. Camping is poor at the lake, and backpackers should look for a site below in the vicinity of the junction. Straddling the western Hoover Wilderness boundary, Anna Peak, 11,144 feet, looms over the lake's bleak setting. It, too, is a nontechnical climb for adept peak baggers.

Trekkers not interested in the short but strenuous side trip to Anna Lake can either return to the parking area or continue on the easy Burt Canyon Trail. In a little over a mile it peters out near the canyon headwall beneath Flatiron Butte. Assess your energy level before heading farther up the canyon. If you're planning to camp, be aware that several black bears live in the canyon. Store food properly to keep the bears wild. The best way to secure your vittles and scented items is in a hard plastic food canister. They are virtually bullet proof and cannot be opened by a bear unless it has a coin or a screwdriver!

2
Molybdenite Creek Canyon
A Gentle Wilderness

◆ THE DETAILS

Getting There: Drive Highway 395 0.7 mile south of Sonora Pass Junction (Highway 108) and turn right (west) on an unpaved Forest Service road signed "Forest Service Campground 3.5 Mi." from the north, "Little Walker River Road" from the south. Trailhead parking is behind site 14 in Obsidian Campground.

Nearest Campground: Obsidian Campground has 14 shaded sites for tents or small RVs spread along Molybdenite Creek. Fee, no piped water, non-reservable, tables, pit toilets. Leashed dogs OK. Open May to October.

Lodging/Services: Walker, 14 miles north, has Andruss Motel 530-495-2166. In Bridgeport, a full service town 16 miles south, try Silver Maple Inn 760-932-7383.

Further Info: Toiyabe National Forest, Bridgeport Ranger District 760-932-7070.

User Groups: Hikers and horses only. Dogs OK on leash.

Hike Distance: 8.8 miles round trip to McMillan Lake, 13.8 miles round trip to end of trail.

Difficulty: Moderate to lake. Because of distance, strenuous to end of trail and back.

Elevation: 7840 feet at trailhead. 9284 feet at McMillan Lake, 9080 feet at end of trail.

Cautions: None.

Best Times to Go: Early summer to late fall.

Map: See page 39.

Other Maps: USFS *Hoover Wilderness Map* or Tom Harrison's *Hoover Wilderness Trail Map* are the best. USGS 7.5-minute topos for Fales Hot Springs, Buckeye Ridge.

Winter Sports: Road may be open and passable in winter, providing opportunities for cross-country skiing and snowshoeing.

OF INTEREST

◆ Close to Burt Canyon and Emma Lake trailheads.

◆ Beautiful wildflowers in early season.

◆ Lightly used trail.

◆ Excellent terrain for horseback riding.

◆ Historic Hunewill Guest Ranch 775-465-2201 (www.hunewillranch.com) has lodging and equestrian packages.

Although stuck with an unmelodious, tongue-twisting moniker, Molybdenite Creek Canyon is blessed with a harmonious convergence of natural features. Easy, pleasant streamside hiking, exquisite spring wildflowers, a showy fall aspen display and amazing specimens of shaggy, thickset Sierra junipers in contrast with sage-studded slopes contribute to a delightful outing.

Not many Eastern Sierra travelers find their way to this beautiful Mono County nook 20 miles northwest of Bridgeport in the Little Walker River drainage. Perhaps because it doesn't have name recognition or because of its unromantic name, surprisingly few hikers know the pleasure of this serene location in a proposed addition to Hoover Wilderness in Toiyabe National Forest.

Similar to neighboring Burt Canyon (see Chapter 1), Molybdenite Creek does not harbor significant historical events. In fact, there is virtually no evidence of past human occupation. Cattle and sheep grazing were once the primary activities in both canyons. Thomas Rickey, a local cattle baron in the 1800s, owned thousands of acres along the Eastern Sierra escarpment. The site of Rickey Cabin can be found about a mile from the trailhead on a ridge west of the path. Near a spring, it once served as a cowboy line shack. Decades ago the Molybdenite Creek area enjoyed a small, brief flurry of molybdenite prospecting, because as with tungsten, a high melting point made it a valuable alloying agent in the production on tempered steel.

A wide, graded dirt road near the junction of Highways 395 and 108 leads 3.5 miles to Obsidian Campground at 7840 feet. It's a pretty forested spot along the creek and an ideal bivouac for Molybdenite and Burt Canyon

Molybdenite Creek tumbles down its verdant course.

Emma Lake near the Little Walker River

day-trippers and backpackers. Obsidian chips in the vicinity offer testimony of former Native American tenancy. Please don't move or remove them. If you're not camping, trailhead parking is behind site 14. There is a wilderness information board, devoid, however, of any information or trail name as of this writing. Flanked by the flowery, aspen-lined creek, the path follows a very mellow grade into the mouth of the canyon. The terrain is crowded with sagebrush and the sunny yellow blooms of mule's ears farther away from the stream. Both plants are ubiquitous in the piñon-juniper woodlands of the Upper Great Basin Sagebrush Steppe.

Sierra junipers, *Juniperus occidentalis var. occidentalis*, aren't strangers to High Country trekkers, but the little colony of geriatric, burly specimens in this much less formidable landscape is an unexpected treat. Typically, they dwell in lofty, austere habitats among domes, cliffs and crags. Firmly anchored in rocky fissures, they abide in extreme climatic conditions where other conifers can't survive. They often live more than 1000 years, and at first glance rather resemble stunted giant sequoias.

Junipers, like the ones here about 2 miles in, never congregate in extensive stands. They live apart from other conifers in small groves or in groups of two or three. Spend some time among them, admiring their spicy aroma, frosty blue berries and muscular cinnamon-red trunks. Some of you may know that the berries are used to flavor gin. Often the beautiful spiral-grained stem is exposed and seems sculpted by a master woodcarver. The squat trunk, whose girth sometimes equals more than its height, appears to be the result of three or four thickly fused coils.

Compared to the many slender, rocky, steep-sided Eastern Sierra canyons, Molybdenite is spacious and open. The tree-clad slopes are significantly less precipitous and more user friendly. The canyon fans out beyond the juniper stand on the border of the proposed wilderness addition, offering terrific views into its peaceful character. The trail never strays far from the creek as it threads the valley between Flatiron Ridge and Hanging Valley Ridge. Bright green in early season and radiant with gold and orange in fall, islands of aspen grace the hillsides. Most hikers will note that the surrounding mountains don't have the characteristic saw-toothed, barren look of Sierra peaks farther to the south. Here, the range is much less jagged and intimidating.

Because of its moderate grade, the trail beckons you to walk on and on to the headwall. Walk as far as you want if there are no time or energy constraints. Any place you decide to turn around makes a rewarding destination. However, if you are goal-oriented, aim for tiny McMillan Lake 4.4 miles from the trailhead. A short, very steep spur trail takes you about 500 yards to the lake. McMillan Lake, elevation 9284 feet, is situated on the west slope of Flatiron Ridge. After circumnavigating the lake's cold waters, linger for awhile and have lunch before retracing your steps.

Continue ambling into the heart of Molybdenite Creek Canyon if you're not yet ready to rejoin civilization. You can travel another 2.5 miles past McMillan Lake spur before the trail ends below Ink Rocks, headwaters for Molybdenite Creek. Though not involving much elevation gain/loss, the 13.8-mile round trip distance is long and can be considered strenuous. For the adventurous and well-conditioned hiker with map and compass skills, it is possible to cross over Hanging Valley Ridge northeast of Walker Mountain and return via Burt Canyon Trail. This is a scenic cross-country jaunt and one of the few loop trips in Hoover Wilderness.

You are well positioned to journey to both Molybdenite and Burt Canyons by staying at Obsidian Campground. A third option from camp is a 3.5-mile drive to Emma Lake Trailhead at road's end. The name supposedly is for Emma Mack, whose parents had a house at the lake in the 1870s. Emma Lake is in a very quiet, lovely alpine setting just 1.2 miles from the car and a peaceful place to spend a few hours or a few days. Mount Emma, the lake's hulking sentinel, will appeal to peak baggers. It's a nontechnical, 1240-foot scramble to the 10,250-foot summit.

Buckeye Canyon
The Journey Is the Destination

◆ THE DETAILS

Getting There: In Bridgeport turn off Highway 395 onto Twin Lakes Road. Follow it for 7.3 miles to an intersection at Doc and Al's Resort. Turn right onto Road 017 and follow the unpaved road 3.4 miles to Buckeye Creek Campground (2.7 miles to junction beyond Buckeye Creek bridge). Drive 0.4 mile through camp to a locked gate blocking vehicular access to Buckeye Creek Trail. Park away from the gate.

Nearest Campground: Buckeye Creek Campground has 65 fee sites, water, flush toilets, tables, fire rings. Dogs allowed on leash. To reach the hot spring, drive 0.4 miles east from the junction of two roads just north of the bridge and park beside the road. A steep path drops a few yards downhill to the spring and a big view of the surrounding area.

Lodging/Services: In Bridgeport, Silver Maple Inn 760-932-7383 is reasonably priced.

Further Info: Toiyabe National Forest, Bridgeport Ranger Station 760-932-7070.

User Groups: Hikers and horses. Dogs OK on leash. No mountain bikes.

Hike Distance: The Forks, 18.8 miles, Big Meadow, 8.2 miles, Wilderness Boundary, 15 miles; Buckeye Pass, 27.6 miles. All distances are round trip.

Difficulty: Moderate to Big Meadow, very strenuous to The Forks because of long round trip distance.

Best Times to Go: Early summer for wildflowers, or autumn for aspen color change.

Cautions: Leave gates as you found them. Stream crossings can be tricky in early season. Start hiking early, temperatures heat up in midsummer.

Elevation: 7200 feet at trailhead, 8469 feet at The Forks.

Other Maps: USGS Buckeye Ridge 7.5-minute topo, Tom Harrison's **Hoover Wilderness Trail Map.** Toiyabe National Forest Map is best for the big picture.

Trip Notes: Dogs allowed on trail. Backpacking permits required for overnight, available at Bridgeport Ranger Station. At press time, the Toiyabe National Forest trail guide for Buckeye Creek incorrectly states the round trip distance to The Forks as 9.4 miles.

Winter Sports: Road may be open and passable in winter, providing opportunities for cross-country skiing and snowshoeing, not to mention hot spring soaking.

OF INTEREST

◆ One of the few Eastern Sierra hikes that has a gentle climb.
◆ The Roughs is a spectacular section of Buckeye Canyon.
◆ Wonderful Buckeye Hot Spring has a lovely setting nearby.

It's rare to hike in the grandeur of Eastern Sierra canyons without having to slog and pant up a steep grade. However, the old saw, "no pain, no gain" does not apply to the mellow trail threading Buckeye Canyon, 12 miles northwest of Bridgeport. An elevation gain of only 1269 feet separate the 9.4 miles between the trailhead at Buckeye Campground and The Forks, translating to 135 feet gain per mile. That's a stroll in the mall, albeit a long one, compared to so many Eastern Sierra treks, especially south of Mammoth Lakes.

Buckeye Creek Trail is one of the least used routes into Hoover Wilderness and the alpine wilds of northeastern Yosemite Park. It offers iris-filled meadows in early season, one of which is two miles-long, spectacular views of rugged Buckeye Ridge and Flatiron Ridge and many appealing places to camp along the creek or around The Roughs. Nearby Buckeye Hot Springs, 1.1 miles from the campground entrance, is a wonderful natural spa to soak your bones after a day on the trail.

Although the hike description guides you 9.4 miles to the merger of the North and South Forks of Buckeye Creek, called The Forks, ramble as far as time and energy dictate. The four-mile, lazy walk as far as Big Meadows is a worthy goal. Buckeye Pass, 4 miles south of The Forks, is best left to marathon-fit walkers or backpackers camping overnight somewhere along the way. Depending on your fitness level, Buckeye Creek Trail can provide hours of easy walking, and except for cattle grazing in the meadows in midsummer, you can expect solitude in this lightly used area.

In addition to day hikes, check the map for several backpacking options. At the bosky confluence of Buckeye Creek forks, turn left (south) to Buckeye

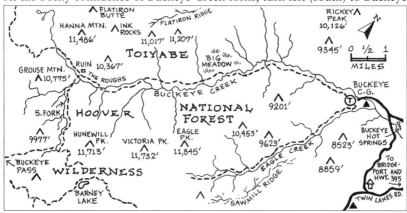

Buckeye Creek with The Roughs in the distance

Pass, elevation 9572 feet, and an infrequently visited backdoor route into Yosemite. Take a right (north) to access destinations in Sonora Pass country. Semi-loop trips requiring shuttles are possible in either direction. A superb 22-mile excursion that travels through a wide variety of Sierra environments can be found between Twin Lakes Trailhead and Buckeye Creek Trailhead.

Buckeye Canyon Trail generally parallels its namesake creek. Although the stream is not always visible, it's never far from the path. The first 2.3 miles trace an old sandy road through sagebrush and scattered stands of Jeffrey pine and aspen. About 200 yards into the hike, a trail to the left leads to the base of Eagle Peak, a strenuous 12-mile round trip. If you have the stamina, add another two miles to the summit for a great vista of the surrounding valleys and peaks.

Don't bother looking for buckeye trees en route because they aren't indigenous in this neck of the woods. All Buckeye place names in the region refer to Buckeye (lumber) Mill Company, originally owned by E. Roberts, perhaps a native of Ohio, the Buckeye State, in the 1860s. For a number of years around the huge gold boom at Bodie, Big Meadow was a noisy, bustling place trying to keep up with the town's ravenous appetite for mining timbers, cordwood and building material.

Napoleon Bonaparte Hunewill bought the Buckeye Mill and timberland, and in 1878 built the Eagle Mill in the lower canyon along the creek by the present-day campground. The "lower mill," as it was known, ran around the clock, turned out 30,000 board feet of lumber per day but couldn't satisfy the demand from Bodie and Bridgeport. Hunewill descendants still own and operate Circle H Ranch not far from Buckeye Canyon.

The first small meadow is overwhelmed with wild iris and many other species of wildflowers in early summer and ringed with junipers and aspens. The road soon dwindles to a trail, reenters forest cover and skirts a larger meadow also starred with flowers. Shortly, dramatic views of Buckeye Ridge, dominated by Eagle, Victoria and Hunewill Peaks, thrust skyward above the soft grasslands. Watch for evidence of beavers around the meadows. Felled aspens displaying sharply gnawed points are telltale signs of their handiwork.

The footpath undulates over a forested ridge, and aptly named Big Meadow comes into sight as you descend to it. It's hard to imagine that this serene, lush setting was once a beehive of industry in the last years of the nineteenth century. At 4.1 miles, wade across Buckeye Creek if you're hiking farther up-canyon. The ford, marked by two posts, can be difficult in May and June. Plan on getting your feet wet. Continue past the meadow on a long traverse up and over a rocky, exposed slope and catch views of the narrowing canyon ahead. A few hundred yards below a saddle on the Hoover Wilderness boundary, you'll need to carefully ford a rowdy, unnamed creek. This is a very scenic rest stop, replete with water music from cataracts above and below the ford.

Past the boundary at 7.5 miles and 8269 feet elevation, the canyon becomes narrower as it passes through a deep granite gorge, reminiscent of Yosemite, shiny with glacial polish. You're now in a stretch called The Roughs where there are two good campsites. Note beaver-downed aspens and the dense trailside forest cover en route to The Forks, 1.7 miles from the wilderness boundary.

The confluence of the North Fork and South Forks of Buckeye Creek is home to a deteriorating cabin. Although the Forest Service did not build it, they used it until the 1950s as a shelter for snow survey personnel. According to a backcountry ranger, it was constructed in the late 1920s, possibly by a shepherd. Across the trail, note the foundation of another structure whose origins and use are unknown to the Forest Service. The old snow survey cabin was originally surrounded by a large meadow, now dense with pines and willows. Thanks to the work of a beaver colony, repeated flooding of the meadow resulted in layers of sediments, and, eventually, a forest replaced the grassland. Backpackers will find good camping spots around the cabin. The old building represents a valuable cultural resource in Toiyabe National Forest. Please respect its antiquity and don't use it for firewood or remove pieces of it for souvenirs.

If you've gone the distance, take a long rest or lunch break and tank up on water. You have another 9.4 miles back to the trailhead. By now, the ambient temperature will be quite warm on the return leg, particularly in the lower canyon. Don't forget to let the hot water of Buckeye Hot Springs (clothes optional) work its magic on your trail-weary muscles before returning to your campsite or driving home.

East Lake

Between every two trees is a door leading to a new life.

~ John Muir

Molybdenite Creek

Reeds and grasses along Green Creek

b

Buckeye Canyon: The Roughs from Big Meadow

East Lake and Epidote Peak

Burt Canyon peaks

Green Lake reflections

Aspens near Conway Summit

Lower Lundy Falls

d

Headwall of upper Lundy Canyon with falls from Burro Lake

Glass Creek Meadow

Parker Lake and its headwall

Molybdenite Creek Canyon

Wildflowers in Lake Canyon

Laurel Canyon headwall and Mammoth Crest

Lundy Canyon

f

Rock Creek Canyon

Rock Creek Canyon near trailhead

Convict Lake

Early morning at Green Creek

Upper McGee Creek Canyon

Long Lake in Rock Creek Canyon

The trail in Pine Creek Canyon

Lower Pine Lake

Ruby Lake near Mono Pass

Tamarack Canyon
In Search Of Serenity

◆ THE DETAILS

Getting There: From Bridgeport on Highway 395 turn west on Twin Lakes Road. Drive approximately 10 miles to where the road enters a 25 mph zone, and turn left onto a dirt road at the "Forest Service Campgrounds" sign. Cross the bridge and continue past Lower Twin Lakes Campground to the trailhead parking area on the right. To find the trail, walk 50 yards back down the road and you'll see a trail sign up to your right.

Nearest Campgrounds: Lower Twin Lakes and Sawmill. Fee, small RVs and tents, piped water, flush toilets, fire grills and tables. Pets on leash OK. To reserve a site at Lower Twin Lakes, call 1-877-444-6777 or go to www.recreation.gov (National Recreation Reservation Service).

Lodging/Services: Bridgeport, a small town with many amenities. Try Hays Street Café for breakfast and lunch. Silver Maple Inn 760-932-7241 or, 6 miles south, Virginia Creek Settlement (excellent dinner menu) 760-932-7780.

Further Info: Toiyabe National Forest, Bridgeport Ranger Station 760-932-7070.

User Groups: Hikers and equestrians. Dogs OK on leash. No mountain bikes.

Hike Distance: (round trip) Tamarack Lake, 9 miles; Hunewill Lake, 11 miles.

Difficulty: Strenuous.

Elevation: 7100 feet at trailhead, 9770 feet at Tamarack Lake, 10,100 feet at Hunewill Lake.

Best Times to Go: Early summer (after snow melt) through October.

Other Maps: USFS **Hoover Wilderness Map**, Tom Harrison's **Hoover Wilderness Trail Map**, or USGS Twin Lakes 7.5-minute or Matterhorn Peak 15-minute topo.

Winter Sports: Twin Lakes Road is generally open and passable in winter, providing opportunities for cross-country skiing and snowshoeing.

OF INTEREST
◆ Good fishing in creek and lakes.
◆ Both lakes have spectacular alpine settings.
◆ Lightly used trail.

A lot of wilderness-loving Californians rush headlong to a mere handful of crowded trailheads leading to popular Sierra hotspots. But, you don't have to be part of the summer stampede. The 400-mile-long Sierra Nevada has an abundance of lonely nooks and crannies where you'll meet few, if any, back-country wayfarers. If you're trolling the map for an unpopulated destination in an out-of-the-way Eastern Sierra location, Tamarack Canyon may be just what you're looking for.

Beaver ponds en route to Tamarack Lake, with Monument Ridge and Crater Crest in background

Tamarack and Hunewill Lakes abide in a rocky basin beneath the abrupt walls of Monument Ridge and Crater Crest in Toiyabe National Forest. Neither lake seems to grab the attention of many hikers and backpackers who enjoy rambling on the sunrise side of the range. Probably because they have almost zero name recognition, the lakes receive only a fraction of the visitors who travel in nearby Green Creek drainage or the Hoover-Virginia Lakes area.

Tamarack Creek cuts through its namesake canyon for 4.5 miles, ending its short journey at Lower Twin Lake a few miles southwest of Bridgeport. Although the lakes are indicated, you won't find Tamarack Canyon marked on modern maps. Not since 1909 has its name appeared on a topo. Except for the first mile, the trail doesn't stray far from the creek.

Beginning at the lower of the two busy Twin Lakes, the 4.5-mile route in-volves a 2600-foot elevation gain to Tamarack Lake, elevation 9770 feet. Add another mile and 330 feet gain to the alpine setting of Hunewill Lake. This is one of those treks where you are not walking in the dense shelter of a deep forest or surrounded by a riotously verdant landscape. Start early because the trail is steep and in full high desert sun most of the way. Remember to chug plenty of water. The long siege of midsummer sun later in the day will rob you of moisture.

After a sharp ascent from the trailhead, the sandy path tops a bench. Catch your breath and take in great views of Sawtooth Ridge, Sawmill Ridge, Lower Twin Lake and Robinson Creek Valley. Still climbing, switchback up another bench and, at just under a mile, crest a moraine at 8000 feet. Stay right at an unsigned junction. Follow the ridgeline for an easy half mile, and enjoy a wide vista of Upper Summers Meadow to the east.

Seasonally, hundreds of sheep inhabit the rich pasture land, a tradition dating back more than a century. The path resumes its climb up a dry, sage-studded slope to Tamarack Creek. Beyond the ford, the trail continues steeply past aspens, scrub trees, sage and bitterbrush into an open, arid, sub-alpine meadow. Look north and east for sweeping views of Bridgeport Valley and the Sweetwater Mountains. The huge blue disk you see is Bridgeport Reservoir not far from the Nevada border.

At 3.5 miles, the trail enters Tamarack Canyon (valley). The steep grade eases here in a lush, marshy area created by a beaver colony. Complete with a pond, the little oasis is a welcome respite from the kiln-dried, high desert environment. A few locals who know of this spot refer to it as "the sloughs" and say fishing for golden trout is good. In early season expect to be greeted by a Luftwaffe of bloodthirsty mosquitoes who also find the oasis to their liking.

A beaver pond is certainly a picturesque sight to come upon. However, North America's largest rodent is not native to this area. In 1941 the Forest Service initiated the first transplant of these husky mammals. Five beaver from Modoc County were placed in Robinson Creek near Bridgeport for the purposes of "water conservation, formation of a fishing lake and more beaver for fur." Here and at other Eastern Sierra waterways, the transplants were very successful, too successful as it turned out.

Bud colonies branched out and set up housekeeping throughout entire drainages and eventually mowed down all the aspens, willows, pines and hardwoods in their forage area. When nearby vegetation was gone, they moved on, leaving behind dead trees killed by flooding, gnawed, pencil-point stumps, and a jumble of debris. Due to limited creekside vegetation in Mono and Inyo Counties, wildlife biologists concluded that the introduction of beaver was a bad idea.

From the pond, it's an easy one-mile walk beneath lodge pole pines and mountain hemlocks. The trail hops the creek and stays on the south side of a pretty meadow. After a moderate rise through a stand of trees, traverse a dry alpine meadow to beautiful Tamarack Lake at 4.5 miles. The large, shallow lake is bounded on two sides by stark, rocky Monument Ridge and on a third side by sloping Crater Crest. Both ridges hold small permanent snowfields. Back-packers will find good places to camp on the north and west sides of the lake.

If you're going the extra mile to Hunewill Lake, elevation 10,100 feet, continue on the trail around Tamarack Lake. From the south end, make your way up the most obvious route around willow thickets and clusters of white-bark pines. Parallel Tamarack's inlet past a tarn up to petite Hunewill's sparse alpine setting at the canyon headwall below 2.5-mile-long Monument Ridge. The lake was named for Napoleon B. Hunewill who operated a sawmill in Buckeye Canyon to the north. A peak and hills also bear his name. Very ex-

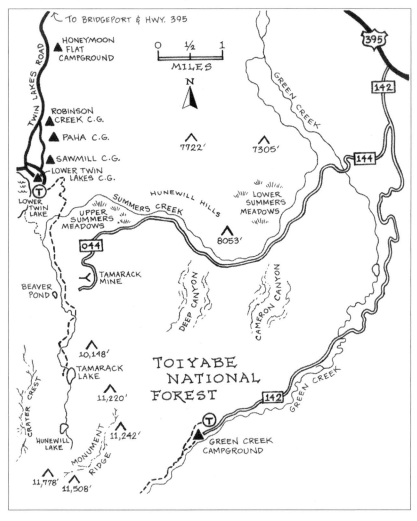

perienced peak scramblers can challenge the ridge, ranging in difficulty from Class 2 to 5, depending on the route.

While taking a break at one of the lakes, you might wonder why this canyon and a lake are named "tamarack." A tamarack is actually an eastern larch, a deciduous conifer that does not grow in California. In the Sierra and other parts of the West, lodge pole pines were erroneously labeled tamaracks. Both species often grow in moist meadows or along stream and lake edges, and perhaps because of this mutual habitat preference, pioneers from the East dubbed them tamaracks.

Tamarack Lake nestles in a meadow beneath Crater Crest.

When you're rested, retrace your boot prints back to Lower Twin Lake. The return journey will give you another perspective of the expansive views you enjoyed on the way up. The hike to Tamarack and Hunewill Lakes should underline that there is much more to the Sierra than its well-trodden landmarks. With just a little effort, one can still find plenty of room to roam in the Sierra Nevada less traveled.

Tamarack and Hunewill Lakes
An Adventurous Alternate Trailhead

◆ THE DETAILS

Getting There: Turn west off Highway 395 4 miles south of Bridgeport onto Green Creek Road. In one mile, turn right onto Summers Meadow Road (Road 144). Follow the directions in this chapter's text from there.

Nearest Campgrounds: Green Creek Campground has 11 sites at the end of Green Creek Road. Fee, small RVs and tents, piped water, vault toilets, fire grill and tables. Pets OK on leash.

Lodging/Services: Bridgeport, a small town with many amenities. Try Hays Street Café for breakfast and lunch. Silver Maple Inn 760-932-7383 or, 6 miles south, Virginia Creek Settlement (excellent dinner menu) 760-932-7780.

Further Info: Toiyabe National Forest, Bridgeport Ranger Station 760-932-7070.

User Groups: Hikers. Dogs OK on leash.

Hike Distance: (round trip from end of road) Tamarack Lake, 6.5 miles; Hunewill Lake, 7.5 miles.

Difficulty: Moderate.

Elevation: 9000 feet at trailhead, 9770 feet at Tamarack Lake, 10,100 feet at Hunewill Lake.

Best Times to Go: Early summer (after snow melt) through October.

Map: See page 52.

Other Maps: USFS **Hoover Wilderness Map**, Tom Harrison's **Hoover Wilderness Trail Map**, or USGS Twin Lakes 7.5-minute or Matterhorn Peak 15-minute topo.

OF INTEREST

◆ The road is an Eastern Sierra equivalent of Mr. Toad's wild ride.

◆ Dramatic views of Bridgeport vicinity and the Eastern Sierra.

◆ Shortest route to two lakes in an alpine setting.

◆ Mining relics and Basque arborglyphs.

Not many visitors know about this offbeat route to two isolated lakes in their serene setting surrounded by Crater Crest and Monument Ridge. The signed trailhead at popular Lower Twin Lake involves a 2600-foot and 3000-foot elevation gain to Tamarack and Hunewill Lakes, 4.5 and 5.5 miles respectively. However, if you're game for 10 adventurous miles of back road through Lower and Upper Summers Meadows, a little known route on Road 144 (which later becomes Road 044) will save about 2.5 hiking miles and a 1900-foot climb to Tamarack Lake. Hikers bound for Hunewill will save 3.5 miles and a 2200-foot gain. Backpackers, especially, will applaud the prospect of less mileage and climbing.

To be honest, this back door approach may not be your idea of a fun time. If slow travel on dirt roads in the boondocks doesn't rev your engine, so to speak, then follow paved Twin Lakes Road to the trailhead (see Chapter 4). The tradeoff for a much shorter and gentler hike into Tamarack Canyon entails driving a lonely Forest Service byway. Autos with sufficient clearance will have no difficulty on the first 6.5 miles. Beyond, a standard SUV or pickup with four-wheel drive is advised.

Except for the last 2.5 miles, which are quite steep and rough, Summers Meadow Road is a good, graded corridor. In return for abandoning the pavement, the dirt track rolls through beautiful high meadows, offering a personal and singular perspective of an Eastern Sierra landscape only hinted at from Highway 395. As you proceed higher, marvelous views of Bridgeport Valley and a brotherhood of peaks along the Sierra Crest delight the eye.

A shade north of State Route 270 to Bodie State Historical Park and 4.4 miles south of Bridgeport, turn west onto Green Creek Road. Set your odometer to zero. After one mile, turn right at signed Summers Meadow Road, Forest Service Road 144. In another mile, cross Green Creek, a lovely, aspen-shaded refuge where you will find a few primitive campsites for tents and

Upper Summers Meadow

small campers. There are no facilities here. Please respect the environment by leaving no evidence of your visit. Pass through Lower Summers Meadow, often inhabited by sheep and a herder in summer, and enter Toiyabe National Forest. The softly rounded, three-mile-long ridge to the right is called Hunewill Hills, named for an 1860s rancher and sawmill operator in the neighborhood.

Approximately 6.4 miles from Highway 395, the road becomes a bit rougher as Upper Summers Meadow drops away on the right. Look left and catch a glimpse of a sagging five-stamp mill in the distance at the site of the old Tamarack Mine Camp. Gold ore from the mine tunnels higher on the mountainside was brought here to be crushed and processed. A side road on the left quickly reaches a good, but primitive, camping area beneath huge aspens.

A spur on the right at 6.6 miles leads to an abandoned shepherd's shack near a spring in an aspen grove. Park off road and take a short walk to the site. Check the trees for arborglyphs, incised designs, made primarily by Basque sheepherders. Sweeping views from the cabin area are very restful and easy on the eye. It's a peaceful, beautiful setting at 8300 feet and worth a few minutes of your time en route to the obscure trailhead. Beyond the shack, the road gets steeper and rougher.

Where the road splits at 6.9 miles, bear right and engage your four-wheel drive. The left fork soon accesses Tamarack Mine Camp. It's private property and occasionally occupied by, presumably, a caretaker or its current owners. The little complex of buildings is in surprisingly good repair. Not much information is extant about the mine, but an inscription on the partially collapsed mill says "Prescott Scott and Co., Union Foundry, San Francisco, 1879."

An old-timer in Bridgeport told me an interesting

Basque-carved arborglyph on an aspen tree

Beaver ponds and meadows along Tamarack Creek

tale about one of the owners. Such tales surrounding mines and miners are invariably fascinating, and this was no exception. According to the story, a miner accumulated $2 million over a period of time. He calculated he had more than enough money to see him through old age, and, for some reason, he decided to dynamite the tunnels shut. Later, elapsed time unknown, he gave a friend permission to mine for gold in his tunnels. The catch was, obviously, clearing away tons of rubble. After some years of unsuccessful labor, the friend gave up. And, like him, we're left wondering if there is still gold in "them thar hills."

Beyond the junction at about 6.9 miles, the rough, sometimes rocky lane continues to climb. Just past 8.2 miles look sharp for a rusty tin shack on the hill to your right that indicates one of the numerous Tamarack Mine works. A short spur leads to it. Two caved-in tunnels, a tailings dump and little piles of ore are all that remain. Another half-mile on the bumpy track brings you to another junction. You're almost there! The left branch is barred by a Forest Service gate. Park near the gate if the last leg of the road seems too daunting to you.

Continue straight ahead on the narrow, steep road that winds through a lodge pole forest and briefly climb a sage-sprinkled slope to a broad, open knoll with terrific vistas of the Bridgeport environs to the north and Sierra Crest to the west. Soon, the road ends, some 9.4 miles from the highway, at a level area beneath lodge pole pines at 9000 feet. Pack it in, pack it out is the golden rule if you're spending the night here or at the view-packed knoll.

From the campsites it is an easy walk to the Tamarack Lake Trail. Head south-southwest up the rocky ridge, which in a few minutes puts you on top. A brief walk brings you to its western edge, below which sparkles a beaver pond. Walk down to it and gain the obvious footpath that leads south to Tamarack and Hunewill Lakes, one and 2 miles distant, respectively. If you have a yen for the road less traveled, as did poet Robert Frost, I think you'll agree that this is the way to visit Tamarack Canyon and its lonely, scenic hinterlands. At day's end, return the way you came.

Horse Creek Canyon
Backcountry Bliss and Dharma Bums

◆ THE DETAILS

Getting There: In Bridgeport turn west on Twin Lakes Road and drive 13 miles to Mono Village at the head of Upper Twin Lake. Parking is available in the boat launch area at no cost for day use, $5 for overnight parking. Just inside the campground entrance, turn left on an old road with a cable across it. Cross Robinson Creek bridge and walk through the woods to a wilderness information signboard. Bear right and you're on your way.

Nearest Campgrounds: Mono Village Resort (private) at Upper Twin Lake has 100 crowded, noisy, shaded sites for RVs and tents. Fee, water, hookups, store and café nearby. First come, first served. Crags Campground has 54 fee sites along Robinson Creek near Twin Lakes. Water, toilets, tables, grills, reservations through www.recreation.gov. Leashed pets OK at both camps.

Lodging: Bridgeport has Silver Maple Inn 760-932-7383, Walker River Inn 760-932-7021 and Ruby Inn 760-932-7241.

Further Info: Bridgeport Ranger District, Toiyabe National Forest 760-932-7070.

User Groups: Hikers. Dogs OK on leash. No mountain bikes.

Hike Distance: 7.6 miles round trip.

Difficulty: Strenuous.

Best Times to Go: Summer, fall.

Cautions: Must hike over rock slides and talus in places. Trail is sometimes vague and very steep past the wilderness boundary.

Elevation: 7092 feet at trailhead, 9500 feet at recommended turn-around point.

Other Maps: USFS *Hoover Wilderness Map* is best—shows all of the 3.8-mile trail. Tom Harrison's *Hoover Wilderness Trail Map* shows the trail only as far as Cattle Creek Trail junction. Or use four 7.5-minute USGS topo maps: Matterhorn Peak, Buckeye Ridge, Dunderberg Peak and Twin Lakes.

Winter Sports: Twin Lakes Road is generally open and passable in winter, providing opportunities for cross-country skiing and snowshoeing.

OF INTEREST

- ◆ Sublime setting below jagged Sawtooth Ridge.
- ◆ Following in footsteps of Jack Kerouac and Gary Snyder.
- ◆ Horsetail Falls and other waterfalls.

◆ Climbing and cross-country opportunities for experienced hikers beyond the main route.

There's no feeling in the world like washing your face in cold water on a mountain morning.　　　　　~Jack Kerouac in *The Dharma Bums*

Horsetail Falls tumbles into rugged Horse Creek Canyon, with Sawtooth Ridge towering above.

Rugged Horse Creek Canyon is a wild piece of Eastern Sierra real estate beneath crenelated Sawtooth Ridge, a magnificent, 3.5-mile-long formation inside Hoover Wilderness. A knife-edged spine (arête) called The Cleaver marks its northwest boundary, and Twin Peaks delineates the upper canyon to the southwest. Roughly in between, massive Matterhorn Peak, elevation 12,264 feet, is an airy, view-packed prize awaiting experienced wilderness travelers and competent climbers.

Horse Creek Canyon Trail is one of my favorite channels into the inner Sierra. Never distant from the creek, the scenery is wild and diverse. Inviting pools, waterfalls, flowers, aspen groves, mixed pine stands, grand Sierra architecture, expansive views, challenging trail and few people add up to pure backcountry bliss. Above it all, the commanding presence of Sawtooth Ridge resembles a line of granite warriors standing guard over the canyon and all who enter.

Until just before the Hoover Wilderness boundary, about 1.85 miles in, the path is defined and not demanding for reasonably fit walkers. However, that changes dramatically as you proceed up-canyon. The trail becomes steadily more challenging and time-consuming. The route is vague or disappears in places as it passes over and around rock slides and talus slopes.

Before going, hikers with a literary bent might want to read or reread *The Dharma Bums* by Jack Kerouac, the Beat Generation's famous voice. The book details a joyous climb of Matterhorn Peak via Horse Creek Canyon in 1955 with Gary Snyder, Pulitzer prize-winning poet. Their journey symbolized a quest for spiritual enlightenment and a search for Buddhist truth, or dharma. Should you follow their footsteps far enough up the trail, you'll see their huge, nearly square, fire-scarred campsite boulder. Even if the Tao of trekking isn't something you ever think about, a hike into Sawtooth country is guaranteed to feed your soul on some level.

Horse Creek Canyon Trail begins at heavily populated Mono Village Resort at the head of 276-acre Upper Twin Lake, 13 miles west of Bridgeport. Don't be annoyed by all the campers, anglers, boaters and general hubbub. You'll soon leave civilization far behind. From the trailhead parking area near the boat launch, walk past the campground entrance kiosk and stay left. Shortly, turn left onto an old road with a cable across it. Proceed to a bridge spanning Robinson Creek. Walk across it and bear right. Soon you'll reach a triangular sign announcing, "Hiking Trail, Closed to All Motorized Vehicles." Mileage for this outing starts here. Stay to the right on a forested trail and cross a tipsy log footbridge.

In 0.5 mile the switchbacking trail climbs to an impressive cascade, incorrectly called Horsetail Falls, crashing over boulders and logs. It's a good Kodak moment and popular destination for casual strollers who vacation at the lake. Beyond, trail usage is light. Past the energetic falls, the route ascends moderately. As you get higher nice views of Upper and Lower Twin Lakes unfold. Each one measures nearly 1.5 miles long, huge bodies of water by Eastern Sierra standards. Approximately one mile above the trailside cataract, the "real" Horsetail Falls, silvery and delicate, slides down a small cliff to the right.

Now on a southerly course, a stunning view of Sawtooth Ridge, known to locals as The Crags, spreads along the horizon. Check the map and see if you can identify the sharp-finned Cleaver. The trail traverses a steep, brushy slope peppered with white fir and aspen. Below, Horse Creek winds through a stand of dead lodge pole pine, victims of flooding caused by beaver activity. Head up canyon past another waterfall. The route climbs again through aspens and tall Jeffrey pines before briefly leveling out near toe-tempting pools along the creek.

Note and walk past a signed intersection for Cattle Creek, .25 mile shy of the wilderness boundary. It's an unmaintained trail heading downhill to Lower Twin Lake. The shady pools are a fine place for a break or a turnaround point. Be advised that before long the Horse Creek route becomes much steeper, rougher and harder to follow. The trail ahead is not suitable for young children.

After the junction, the trail remains fairly level for awhile in a mixed forest before penetrating a brushy, damp section that can be a difficult bushwhack in early season. You'll now have to contend with the first big rock slide, beyond which is an open area amidst large boulders. Many species of flowers linger here until September in years of average precipitation. Less adventurous and/or less fit visitors will probably choose to turn around at this point. The Hoover Wilderness boundary sign marks the Sawtooth Ridge area. Maximum group size is limited to eight backpackers, and no campfires are permitted.

Put your legs in a lower gear and take it easy through the slide where the use trail vanishes in places. The best way to cross the slide is to stay above the line where the rocks meet the willows. Always look ahead to pick out the trail whenever it seems to disappear beneath the boulders. Take notice of a side creek flowing down the

western wall before joining Horse Creek. Currant bushes, laden with red berries in autumn, and purple, aromatic pennyroyal, dot the eastern slope.

Your steep hike segues to really steep as you clamber across rock slides and talus. Yet another waterfall plunges over a rock wall blocking the climb up the narrow gorge. You'll have to contend with a long, steep grind straight uphill along the edge of the slide to the top of a terminal moraine. A few campsites can be found on a heather-clad bench where fierce winds and snowstorms have sculpted mountain hemlocks into ground-hugging, Bonsai-like creations, termed Krummholz by botanists. The Dharma Bums' gigantic boulder and camp are about .25 mile upstream on the far end of a plateau.

Timberline trees have to be tough. They live on the edge of life, enduring severe winters, dry summers, poor soil and a very short growing season at high elevation. Krummholz provides a good lesson in survival. The diminutive trees are masterpieces of adaptation to an extreme environment. Their reduced size allows them to sustain life where larger trees cannot.

From atop the bench, you'll groan at the sight of another barrier in the form of a small ridge cutting across the canyon floor between you and a full view of Sawtooth Ridge. Descend to the valley floor, strewn with boulders and downed trees, although a few live ones march along the stream. Determined, well-conditioned hikers comfortable in timberline situations can continue on an even more demanding route up a narrow cleft to access 10,700-foot Horse Creek Pass, known to climbers but unnamed on maps.

The pass is a notch to the southwest at the head of a Horse Creek tributary. Also unnamed on maps, Horse Creek Peak is an 11,600-foot sentinel perched above the col to your left. A rock-bound tarn nearby glitters in its austere, alpine world. Atop Sawtooth Ridge, absolutely stupendous views of Matterhorn Peak and its remnant glaciers, The Cleaver and far-distant Bridgeport Valley will leave you speechless and wide-eyed.

Stalwart hikers and climbers who make it as far as Horse Creek Pass will find a number of hard-core options to choose from. Experienced mountaineers can ascend the Matterhorn's Class 2 southeast or southwest side, first climbed in 1899. A cross-country jaunt down lonesome Spiller Creek to a junction with the Tahoe-Yosemite Trail will appeal to others. A really tough circumnavigation of Sawtooth Ridge via a trailless Class 3 crossing of Whorl Mountain-Matterhorn Ridge to Burro Pass eventually leads back to Upper Twin Lake. CAUTION: THESE ARE NOT VIABLE OPTIONS FOR THE AVERAGE HIKER.

This 3.8-mile trail description into pristine Horse Creek Canyon ends at 9500 feet at the point where the trail veers away from the canyon to the right (southwest) and switchbacks up to Horse Creek Pass. However, hikers should stop whenever they feel the route is exceeding their physical limits. If you're strictly destination oriented, no matter what the cost, you're probably not going to enjoy the journey. Walking a High Country trail is often demanding and calls for much more endurance, cardio output and leg strength than most of us use in everyday life.

Hiking, after all, should be a joyful experience, not a "forced march" that reduces you to a rubbery-legged, whining, wheezing, miserable person. When you sense the route is becoming too much of a challenge and you are no longer having fun, pay attention to that little voice inside telling you to stop. It's time to take a break, rest, have a snack and a cool drink of water. When rested, you might choose to continue, or to return to the trailhead.

I myself'd gotten the water from the stream, which was cold and pure like snow and the crystal-lidded eyes of heaven. ~Jack Kerouac

A beaver dam along lower Green Creek

Green Creek Canyon
A Fistful of Lakes and High Visual Drama

◆ THE DETAILS

Getting There: Turn west off Highway 395 onto Green Creek Road, 4 miles south of Bridgeport and about 3 miles north of State Route 270 to Bodie. Follow Green Creek Road 8.6 miles to trailhead parking.

Nearest Campgrounds: Green Creek Campground, 0.2 mile beyond the trailhead has 11 sites with piped water, open May through October. Free, primitive camping can be found along Green Creek in the last mile before the trailhead.

Lodging: Two miles south of Green Creek Road, Virginia Creek Settlement 760-932-7780 has several rustic rooms in an old west mining camp setting. Bridgeport has Ruby Inn 760-932-7241, Cain House 760-932-7040, Silver Maple Inn 760-932-7383.

Further Info: Bridgeport Ranger District, Toiyabe National Forest 760-932-7070.

User Groups: Hikers and horses. Dogs OK on leash. No mountain bikes.

Hike Distance: (all round trip) 4.8 miles to Green Lake, 7.6 miles to West Lake, 7.6 miles to East Lake, 9.6 miles to Gilman Lake, 11.2 miles to Hoover Lakes, 15.2 miles to Summit Lake.

Difficulty: Moderate to strenuous, depending on distance.

Best Times to Go: July, early August for wildflowers, September or early October for fall color.

Cautions: Use caution at stream fords, possibly impassable in early season.

Elevation: 8160 feet at trailhead. Gain to Green Lake: 800 feet. Gain to East Lake: 1340 feet. Gain to Summit Lake: 2040 feet.

Other Maps: USFS *Hoover Wilderness Map* and/or Tom Harrison's *Hoover Wilderness Trail Map*, USGS Dunderberg Peak 7.5-minute topo.

Winter Sports: Road may be open and passable in winter, providing opportunities for cross-country skiing and snowshoeing.

OF INTEREST

◆ Canyon of many delights, even if you don't venture beyond the end of the road.

◆ Great canyon for wildflowers.

◆ Abundant aspen stands offer brilliant autumn color.

◆ Trail offers a choice of numerous gorgeous lakes in a colorful setting.

◆ Site of first long-distance electrical transmission in the world.

Veteran hikers and backpackers know that 8.6-mile-long Green Creek Road provides entry to several sparkling High Country lakes in lightly traveled Hoover Wilderness and access to Yosemite Park's secluded northeastern backcountry. After the dirt road passes a lakelet around 3 miles in, it cleaves the narrow canyon cut by Green Creek. During July and early August the landscape is vibrant with wildflowers, while thick stands of aspens produce brilliant color displays in autumn.

An outing into Green Creek's magnificent backcountry will appeal to a broad mix of interests. Depending on your fitness level, there are many destinations to choose from. Day hikers, anglers, backpackers, shutter bugs and botany and geology buffs will be immensely satisfied by a trip to one or more of the lakes. Backpackers can put together out and back trips or long shuttle trips into northeastern Yosemite's lonesome Matterhorn Canyon from Green Creek's 8160-foot trailhead.

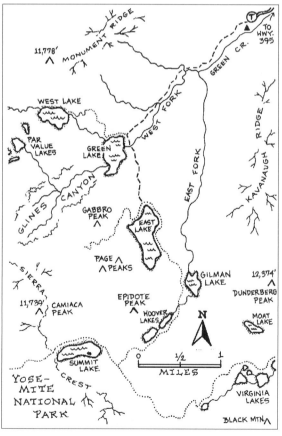

As well as a tranquil, lovely subalpine setting, the picturesque lakelet at the slender valley's entrance harbors a piece of revolutionary history whose significance rippled far beyond this tiny Sierra side road. Dynamo Pond's log-cribbed outlet and a few ruins are all that remain of a hydroelectric plant constructed in 1892 to supply power to the mines at Bodie.

Big, bad Bodie was one of the wildest, wickedest, richest and largest gold camps in the West. At its peak between 1877 and 1882, Bodie claimed 10,000 residents, and its mines yielded $35 million in gold and silver. Although the boom was ephemeral and most of the mines closed permanently by 1890, the Standard Company continued as Bodie's main producer until 1942.

Prior to 1892, energy for the mills was derived from steam generated by wood-fired boilers. A single mining company could consume 24 cords of wood per day. Over the years, Bodie's insatiable appetite for lumber, mine timbers, and cordwood for heating and machine operations resulted in a critical shortage. Tremendous quantities of wood were needed to simply survive long and nasty winters. For example, in late 1878 more than 18,000 cords of piñon pine were stockpiled awaiting the first cold snap. In 1882, five million board feet of lumber and 27,000 cords of firewood were hauled to Bodie.

As wood fuel became increasingly scarce and more costly, the Standard Company's chief engineer and superintendent, Tom Legget, proposed that electricity could be transmitted by wires to any distance. This was a radical concept because electricity had only been used where it was generated. After many meetings with company stockholders, he was granted permission to construct a power plant. Green Creek Canyon, eight miles south of Bridgeport, was selected as the nearest site with a reliable water source.

The Standard Company created Dynamo Pond by building a log-cribbed dam to capture Green Creek's flow, providing water to generate electricity in the plant below it. Capable of developing 6600 volts and 130 horsepower, Dynamo Pond was ready for a test in November 1892. Skeptics dubbed the project "Legget's Folly," and many stockholders believed the Company was wasting money on project construction, new equipment to replace steam-powered machinery, and the mill's closure to retrofit for electrical operation.

Meanwhile, the company ordered surveyors to install power poles in a perfectly straight line because it was feared that electricity could not turn corners and would "fall off the line and fly into space." A telephone line was built parallel to the power line. In spite of the scoffing from skeptics, the experimental 13-mile power line from Dynamo Pond to Bodie successfully carried the first long-distance transmission of electricity in history.

The unprecedented achievement at Bodie revolutionized the use of electricity in industry. News of the engineering breakthrough quickly spread around the world. Tom Legget soon became a famous man, in demand to build similar hydroelectric plants in the United States and as far away as Rhodesia and Australia. Ironically, residents of Bodie did not enjoy the benefits of electricity until 1910 when the population had dwindled to a few hundred.

Don't be fooled by the rather desolate, uninviting entrance to Green Creek Canyon. Three miles up the road at historic Dynamo Pond, the barren hillsides give way to a moist, beautifully vegetated gorge that invites lingering. Lake hopping in Hoover Wilderness provides hikers with highly scenic, memorable excursions. Campers can stay at a small Forest Service campground near the end of the road. You'll find the trailhead on the road's other spur nearby.

The trail follows the wooded canyon floor, passing a spring that flows down from the right. Your gentle track steepens after 0.5 mile, ascends a rocky ridge, and then climbs switchbacks to follow West Fork Green Creek. Enter Hoover Wilderness around one mile and draw near the noisy, frothy creek. Catch sight of volcanic Gabbro Peak ahead and granitic Monument Ridge to the right. Note the work of busy aspen-gnawing beavers along here.

Hikers accustomed to the characteristic white and gray granite found in most eastside canyons will be surprised by the multicolored peaks in Green Creek drainage. There is nothing subtle about this scenery. The trinity of Gabbro, Page and Epidote Peaks dazzles the eye with crimson, terra cotta and carnelian hues. These startling shades are all the more intense in contrast with the sedate black of metavolcanic rock.

Another moderate climb reveals a view on your right of the stream tumbling down from West Lake. More switchbacks bring you to a junction just below Green Lake by 2.3 miles. This described hike takes the left fork, but consider a short side trip to Green Lake, a stunning emerald jewel only 0.2 mile from the junction. The right fork skirts the north shore of Green Lake past campsites and a sweeping vista of Glines Canyon rising toward Virginia Pass on the Sierra Crest. Green Lake, rimmed with forest and wildflowers, is a great location for a snack break before tackling more switchbacks. Another trail heads north from a lakeshore junction, gaining 900 feet in elevation to reach West Lake at 3.8 miles.

Below the trailhead, Green Creek's still pools reflect the jagged peaks up-canyon.

Another option available from Green Lake's

Sierra junipers cling to the rocky slopes above Green Lake.

superb environs is a steep trip to Virginia Pass on the Yosemite boundary. A use trail alongside the inlet heads up infrequently traveled Glines Canyon to the 10,500-foot summit. However, it's a journey only veteran, hardy hikers should tackle. The average day-tripper will probably not be tempted to take on the 200-foot headwall and semi-permanent snowfield just below the pass. Nevertheless, even a short walk up this rarely visited rugged canyon and its lush, willow-dotted meadows offers hikers a deeper appreciation of gorgeous Green Creek Basin.

From the junction below Green Lake, take the left fork and dip across the lake's outlet stream. The ford may be difficult, even impassable, during high water runoff. Beyond the ford, follow the trail as it climbs steeply south heading for East Lake. Part way up you veer east to cross East Lake's outlet, then loop away from the creek before returning to it for two more fords. Notice the outlet's small flood-control dam, another remnant of Bodie's power works.

Just below East Lake's 9458-foot outlet, the trail passes through a lovely flower-filled meadow. Top a rise around 3.8 miles to find 75-acre East Lake twinkling beneath multihued Gabbro, Page and Epidote Peaks. Views of these colorful mountains over the lake's cobalt-blue waters are sublime. This is a postcard perfect spot to lunch while you soak up the exquisite scenery. It's also a splendid base camp for sorties to nearby West, Nutter, Gilman, Hoover and Summit Lakes.

Conditioned Sierra stompers, however, should consider continuing up the lake-blessed drainage to Summit Lake, elevation 10,200 feet, 3.8 miles ahead. En route, pass beautiful little Nutter Lake before reaching a faint lateral trail down to resplendent Gilman Lake at 4.8 miles. Gilman, with its lush meadow and forest cover at the base of massive Dunderberg Peak, is a photographer's dream. Because it's off trail, hikers and campers will find plenty of solitude.

Past the unmarked spur, the route fords the stream between Gilman Lake and Hoover Lakes before climbing sharply to Hoover Lakes at 9819 feet. The lakes are small and sit on a bench between the moody darkness of Epidote Peak and the rich red rock of a nameless mountain to the southeast. Ford the stream between the lakes, cross upper Hoover's inlet, and hike steeply beside Summit Lake's outlet.

At 6.3 miles, ignore a left-hand trail to Virginia Lakes (see Chapter 8), and proceed on a moderate grade to Summit Lake. Straddling the crest, its waters flow down both sides of the Sierra. Enjoy the incomparable grandeur of alpine scenery and superb views at this magnificent, half-mile-long lake before retracing your steps 7.6 miles to the trailhead. Backpackers take note that Summit Lake is generally a very windy location and much of the shoreline is closed to camping due to the fragility of the vegetation. Find a campsite somewhere else.

Azure Hoover Lakes sit below massive Dunderberg Peak.

8
Virginia Lakes Canyon
A Lake-Filled Trek to Burro Pass

◆ THE DETAILS

Getting There: From Highway 395 at Conway Summit, 13.5 miles south of Bridgeport, turn west onto Virginia Lakes Road. Drive 6 miles past a pack station to the trailhead at Big Virginia Lake day-use area, where toilets and water are available.

Nearest Campgrounds: Trumbull Lake Campground at 9500 feet, near the trailhead, has 45 shaded, fee sites for tents and RVs with water, fire rings, tables and vault toilets. Leashed pets OK. Open mid-June to mid-October. Some sites can be reserved through www.recreation.gov. A trail from the campground leads to Blue Lake. Free, primitive camping along Virginia Creek on Forest Service Road 139. Turn left off Virginia Lakes Road 2.4 miles or 4.8 miles up from the highway.

Lodging: Virginia Lakes Resort 760-647-6484 for reservations. In Bridgeport try Silver Maple Inn 760-932-7383.

Further Info: Bridgeport Ranger District, Toiyabe National Forest 760-932-7070.

User Groups: Hikers and horses. Dogs OK on leash. No mountain bikes.

Hike Distance: 6.6 miles, round trip, to Burro Pass.

Difficulty: Moderately strenuous.

Best Times to Go: Summer, fall.

Cautions: Go slowly, pause often if you are not acclimated.

Elevation: 9700 feet at trailhead, 11,150 feet at Burro Pass.

Other Maps: USGS Dunderberg Peak 7.5-minute topo, Tom Harrison's ***Hoover Wilderness Trail Map***, USFS ***Hoover Wilderness Map*** or Toiyabe National Forest Map.

OF INTEREST

◆ Three easily accessible lakes.

◆ Many more lakes for those who hike up the canyon.

◆ Abundant waterfalls and wildflowers.

Virginia Lakes are cupped in a striking setting on the edge of Hoover Wilderness between the formidable ramparts of 12,374-foot Dunderberg Peak to the north and 11,800-foot Black Mountain to the south. A chain of ten alpine lakes,

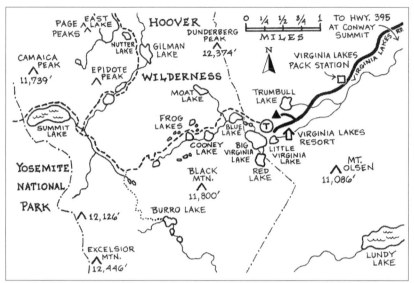

a profusion of summer wildflowers, brilliant fall color and exhilarating scenery mitigate the strenuous climb to Burro Pass. From the 11,150-foot high point, a smorgasbord of options will tempt long-distance day hikers, backpackers and experienced peak baggers. For either the neophyte or seasoned backcountry traveler, this outing offers a first-rate sampling of High Country grandeur.

The hike begins at the hikers' parking area near Big Virginia Lake, six miles west of Highway 395. Paved Virginia Lakes Road offers a beautiful drive up canyon, particularly in early October when vast stands of aspen don their fall finery. The road forks past the pack station. To the left you'll find a small lodge, store and café, and to the right is Trumbull Lake Campground. Proceed to the signed trailhead at the end of the road.

Don't be put off by the number of cars and people you may see here, especially on summer weekends. For many decades little Virginia Lakes Resort has been a beloved place for people to vacation in the rustic cabins, fish and watch the pine trees grow. It's also a popular trailhead, but most users are casual walkers and don't stray very far from Big Virginia Lake. To illustrate, a grumbling middle-aged gentleman complained to me that "they built the trail too damn steep and even at bayonet point I couldn't be made to walk it!" His comments underline that adjectives like steep, easy and strenuous are relative in the eyes of the beholder. Mountain hiking is as much about attitude as it is about physical condition.

Forested at the beginning, the trail climbs moderately around lovely Blue Lake, less than one-half mile from the trailhead. Note its inlet streams crashing down the slopes from Cooney and Moat Lakes. The dry talus slope above the 9886-foot lake is home to an impressive flower display. It also provides lodging for colonies of pikas, or rock rabbits. These industrious little critters spend the entire summer harvesting grass to store in their burrows for winter munching. With a mouthful of grass, they appear to sport big green whiskers. Before leaving Blue Lake, take a minute to marvel at the colorful landscape surrounding its azure waters—burgundy red Dunderberg Peak, dark Black Mountain, cobalt sky, white snow fields, and deep green thickets of trees. It's truly an eye-filling landscape.

At 0.75 mile the rocky trail crosses unseen Moat Lake's outlet. If you have the time and energy for a rigorous half-mile jaunt to a secluded lake, clamber up the steep use trail paralleling the stream. The views are fantastic from pristine Moat Lake. You just may choose to spend the day here as I did on my first visit to the canyon. Otherwise, continue the ascent past a lush, flower-decked meadow and through forest cover before arriving at a well-preserved old cabin built by a miner named Cooney at one mile. Thoughtful wilderness users will leave artifacts in place for others to enjoy.

Growing more steeply now, a quarter-mile climb brings you to the stunning north shoreline of Cooney Lake at 10,246 feet. This is a very scenic place for a snack break on the rocks above the lake. From this austere timberline location, Burro Pass on the western skyline comes into view. Beyond Cooney the path switchbacks steeply up to Frog Lakes, a cluster of small lakes, the largest of which is five acres. Yellow-legged frogs live in its icy waters 1.8 miles from the trailhead.

If you can't find Burro Pass, the destination of this hike description, on any map, don't fret. Though the barren, windy summit is officially unrecognized, locals have long referred to it as Burro Pass. The "real" Burro Pass is far away to the northwest below Matterhorn Peak. It's also marked incorrectly as Summit Pass on the handout available at Virginia Lakes Store.

Leave the three lakelets and resume climbing sharply over a series of rocky benches. The terrain loses its stunted tree cover and becomes increasingly more alpine as you ascend the north cirque wall. Here at timberline the mineral-rich soil hosts an amazing crop of high elevation wildflowers. Pass a nameless tarn on your left before laying into a final set of switchbacks to Burro Pass on the canyon headwall at 3.3 miles. From the 11,500-foot summit, actually a wide, flat bench, a vista to the east over Virginia Lakes Basin is more than enough to blow out your

Sinuous young aspens

Summit Lake area above Frog Lakes in Virginia Creek Canyon

visual circuit breakers.

But you don't need to stop here. After catching your breath, walk a couple of minutes northwest to a rocky outcrop on the right and gape at the simply astounding, dramatic panorama of the Sawtooth Range on the Sierra Crest and Hoover and East Lakes in Green Creek Canyon. Besides the big picture, be sure to appreciate the wee alpine flowers living among the colorful, lichen-splashed metamorphic rocks. Linger awhile before retracing your steps.

While in the vicinity, consider Burro Pass as a good launch pad for hard-core hikers comfortable with cross-country travel and map/compass skills who would enjoy the challenge of summiting Black Mountain. The 11,800-foot peak is a Class 2 climb from the north and south sides. Another very strenuous option is to maneuver over Black Mountain's west flank down to Burro Lake, elevation 10,547 feet. The difficult terrain requires hikers to be as strong, sure-footed and nimble as bighorn sheep. Burro Lake and several lakelets sit in isolated splendor in a beautiful little glacial valley at the base of Excelsior Mountain. To describe the lake as remote is truly an understatement. Burro Lake, whose outlet stream cascades into Lundy Canyon, has that rarely seen, milky turquoise hue characteristic of glacial lakes.

It's been said that passes have a way of separating casual strollers from serious hikers. To avid mountain trekkers, passes are sirens, seducing them to proceed ever higher and deeper into the inner Sierra. Burro Pass is indeed a portal to a variety of wild and remote backcountry. Generally, passes are mostly crossed by backpackers traveling to locations far off the beaten path. Fortunately, Burro Pass is relatively close to the trailhead, and its dramatic timberline beauty is available to reasonably fit day hikers. Few trails this short offer such a wealth of scenery, and you'll get to enjoy most of it a second time as you head back down the canyon.

9
Lundy Canyon
Gem of the Eastern Sierra

◆ THE DETAILS

Getting There: From the junction of Highway 395 and Highway 167, seven miles north of Lee Vining, turn west onto signed, paved Lundy Lake Road and drive 5 miles into the mountains. To find Lake Canyon Trailhead, turn left on a spur road just below the lake's outlet and drive 0.2 mile to the locked gate and trailhead. To reach upper Lundy Canyon Trailhead, drive about 2 miles farther up the road to its end beyond the little resort complex.

Nearest Campground: Lundy Lake Resort (private) has 35 sites with piped water, open May to October while Mill Creek Campground (Mono County), just below Lundy Lake, has 54 fee sites, open May to October, no piped water, toilets, pets OK, tables, fire rings.

Lodging: Lundy Lake Resort 626-309-0415, Box 550, Lee Vining, CA 93541, has basic housekeeping cabins. In Lee Vining, try Lake View Lodge 760-647-6543.

Further Info: Stop at the visitor information center in Lee Vining or at the Mono Basin Visitor Center 760-647-3044, one mile north of town for maps, books, displays and specific information.

User Groups: Hikers. Dogs OK on leash. No mountain bikes.

Hike Distance: (all round trip) Lake Canyon: 3 miles to canyon, 7 miles to Oneida Lake and May Lundy Mine. Lundy Canyon Trailhead to Lower Lundy Falls: 1.2 miles, 3 miles to cabin, 5 miles to base of Upper Lundy Falls, 6 miles to Lake Helen. It is also possible to do a 6.75-mile shuttle hike to Saddlebag Lake Trailhead beyond the top of Lundy Canyon—arrange a shuttle before you go.

Difficulty: Strenuous to Oneida Lake. Moderate to very strenuous, depending on stopping point, to top of Upper Lundy Falls.

Best Times to Go: Summer for wildflowers and waterfalls, autumn for incredible aspen foliage display.

Cautions: Leave mining relics and other historical artifacts where you find them. If you hike to the Tioga Crest, use the utmost caution and good sense traveling on the exposed segment of trail and through the loose talus slope just below the top.

Elevation: 7800 feet at Lake Canyon Trailhead, 8200 feet for Lundy Canyon Trailhead, 9700 feet at Oneida Lake, 10,000 feet at Tioga Crest/Lake Helen.

Other Maps: Inyo National Forest Map, Tom Harrison's **Hoover Wilderness Trail Map** or USGS 7.5-minute topos for Dunderberg Peak and Lundy.

OF INTEREST

◆ Among the Eastern Sierra's most stunning canyons.

◆ Abundant mining history and relics.

◆ Waterfalls and abundant wildflowers.

◆ Glorious autumn color.

◆ Possible shuttle hike to Saddlebag Lake.

◆ Near dramatic Mono Lake, which has good canoeing and kayaking.

Cruising along Highway 395 below the abrupt, bony spine of the Eastern Sierra escarpment, most travelers are so enchanted by the striking vista across Mono Lake Basin that they pass by Lundy Canyon, unaware of one of the region's most stunning settings. Follow the sign pointing up Lundy Canyon for a highly scenic side road and trailhead parking. Pretty in any season, in late September and early October when autumn paints the landscape with startling shades, this glacially sculpted canyon is unrivaled.

This is a place not to be rushed. The more time you spend in the tranquil, secluded gorge, the more you'll be rewarded. Stay a few days to fully explore the Lundy environs. Before reaching Lundy Lake, elevation 7700 feet, you'll find a public campground along aspen- and willow-lined Mill Creek. Above the lake is a tiny rustic resort with a store and campground.

At this idyllic mountain getaway, you won't find the usual hustle of more commercial resorts where throngs of people mill around waiting to be entertained. Instead, Lundy radiates a peaceful, unsophisticated and low-key charisma. The big attraction is simply the landscape. You'll find all the entertainment you need hooking a huge trout, hiking up the forks of the canyon past shimmering lakes and roaring waterfalls, watching a hawk ride a thermal, feeling the cool caress of night breezes and smelling the spicy scent of Jeffrey pines.

Two lovely trails through the remarkably photogenic region beg for your boots. They offer riots of wildflowers in summer and especially dazzle in autumn when aspens flaunt intense orange and lemon hues. The farther up you proceed, the more dramatic the pageant becomes. You'll be surrounded by the aspens' glorious display, intensified by the deep green pines and the red-walled cliffs. Rivers of quaking gold tumble down the canyon walls for hundreds of feet.

Part of Lundy's appeal, besides its rugged beauty, is its rich history, dating back more than 125 years to the exciting days of pioneers and boisterous mining activity. Not much of the old town remains, but relics from the past are everywhere: rusting tramways, tunnels, abandoned trails and mining paraphernalia. Collapsed buildings and decaying mills are scattered throughout the area.

About 1878 William Lundy started a sawmill in the canyon to satisfy the need for prodigious quantities of firewood and mine timbers in Bodie, a booming gold rush town northeast of here. In 1879, a year of intense activity for Bodie and Mammoth Lakes, William Wasson discovered veins of ore in Mill Creek, now Lundy Canyon. That same year Lundy and his two partners established claims, among them the famous May Lundy, named after one of his four daughters.

The May Lundy Mine, located on a stark, sheer slope above 10,000 feet in Lake Canyon, 3.5 miles south of Lundy, was worked continuously from 1878 to 1898. The town burst into existence by May 1880 and boasted 500 inhabitants. According to its newspaper, the **Homer Mining Index**, "During that month upward of thirty frame houses, nearly all for business purposes, were built, besides a number of log houses, two merchandise stores, seven saloons, two lodging houses, several boarding houses, two bakeries, a hotel, blacksmith shop, livery stable, assay office, butcher shop, post office, express office, sawmill and a newspaper." Not bad for a newborn town. A telegraph line to Bodie, and later to Bennettville, connected Lundy to the outside world.

The Lundy Mining Company built a large store with several bedrooms upstairs. The first stamp mill was across from the store, and the ore was laboriously toted down from the May Lundy by mules and horses. When a toll road was established in 1881 connecting Lundy to the mine in Lake Canyon, the mill was moved up to the ore site. The difficulty in negotiating the steep road from the mine stimulated development of "three saloons, a laundry and two boarding houses" at nearby Crystal Lake. Business was brisk as men from Bennettville nine miles south also used Lundy's "conveniences."

Strike from your mind the romantic Hollywood image of a gold seeker lazily swishing gravel around in a gold pan. Life was a labor intensive, dangerous business for hard-rock miners in this oxygen-scarce, rugged terrain. During long and brutally cold winters, the crude living quarters offered little comfort or protection from months of raging winds and tremendous snow accumulation. Like most mining camps, Lundy had plenty of colorful characters, murders and robberies. On top of daily hardships, whiskey and boredom often combined to shorten tempers and cloud judgments.

An important, but fleeting, relationship between Lundy and Bennettville mining camps provides an astonishing example of the courage, tenacity and ingenuity of hard-rock miners. These men attempted or accomplished many extraordinary feats, and the following story illustrates one such mind-boggling venture in their quest for precious metals.

Before the Great Sierra Wagon Road, forerunner of Tioga Road, was built, only the treacherous Bloody Canyon-Mono Pass Trail (see Chapter 13) afforded access to Bennettville, headquarters for the Tioga Mining District. In 1881 owners of the Great Sierra Silver Mine constructed an even steeper trail from Lake Canyon above Lundy town to Bennettville over the Sierra Crest. Its purpose was to transport heavy-duty machinery necessary to drive a tunnel 1000 feet through granite so hard it took several shifts of miners to drill a single blast hole.

Arriving at Lundy from San Francisco via Reno, the lighter equipment was packed on mules and sent to Bennettville over the Bloody Canyon Trail. However, the more ponderous cargo consisting of an engine, boiler, air compressor, iron pipe and drills far exceeded the animals' capabilities. Instead, 16,000 pounds of machinery were hauled over the new trail by, if you can imagine, sleds in the dead of winter in 1882!

After loading six huge hardwood sleds built at Lundy, twelve men began the Herculean labor of dragging eight tons of equipment 4000 feet up to the summit and then down to Bennettville. The heaviest load was 4200 pounds. Two mule-powered bobsleds carried supplies. Aided only by nearly a mile of manila rope and block and tackle snubbed to nearby trees or steel bars pounded into rocks, a dozen men snaked the gear over cliffs, frozen lakes and icy talus slopes. Costing one man his life, the task required two months to drag the colossal load a distance of nine miles.

In a classic understatement, company manager J.C. Kemp remarked at the end of the journey, "It's no wonder that men grow old." The trail continued to be used by pedestrians and pack trains carrying dynamite and supplies until mining operations closed in summer 1884. Today, hardy High Country hikers occasionally enjoy the rarely used route in search of solitude and magnificent scenery.

Weather was always a critical factor in the story of Lundy. Then as now, winters were severe. Avalanches posed a constant threat and resulted in much devastation and loss of life throughout the years. When miners first built their cabins, they didn't realize the potential disaster of building the town at the base of barren, towering mountains. The winter of 1882 was particularly vicious. After days of monumental snowfall, three avalanches thundered down Mount Scowden, buried most of the town and killed several people. The dead were laid to rest in a little cemetery below the lake, scarcely visible since the fences around the graves have weathered away.

Besides mining activity, Lundy had several farms below the lake that were irrigated by diverting water from Mill Creek. The farms' produce found an eager market in Lundy and Mono Basin. The town also had at least three sawmills along the creek. These mills virtually denuded the area of trees in supplying firewood and mine timbers.

By the turn of the twentieth century, the glory years were nearly over, even though Lundy hung on for awhile longer. The May Lundy was a major producer in the district, reportedly taking out more than $2 million in gold during its twenty years of production. Harsh winters, economic upheavals, fires, avalanches and depletion of gold veins led to the demise of this once thriving community. Although intermittent mining has continued on a small scale, very little success is evident. Production costs are simply too great to make it a truly profitable endeavor.

◆ THE HIKES

Today's visitor doesn't have to leave the car—or stray far from it—to enjoy Lundy's gifts, but the best way to immerse yourself in the glorious landscape is to take a walk on one or both of two choice trails.

The highly scenic and historic hike to May Lundy Mine requires a very steep climb up Lake Canyon. The signed trailhead is at the lower end of mile-long Lundy Lake near the dammed outlet. Abounding with rugged beauty and mining relics, the route traces the old mining toll road and passes three lakes. The trail reaches Lake Canyon around 1.5 miles and swings south to follow South Fork Mill Creek upstream through the forest. Stay alert for remnant poles of the 123-year-old telegraph line above the road to the right.

South Lake Canyon Falls

After crossing the creek on a culvert at 2 miles, watch for the grade to taper off a bit before another steep ascent. Straight ahead Doré Cliffs on the Tioga Crest pop into view. The trail levels out again in a wet meadow. On its way to becoming a meadow, look for tiny Blue Lake on the left. The old road soon forks. Stay to the right unless you want to investigate the site of Wasson town around the shoreline of Crystal Lake where May Lundy miners lived in the 1880s. The ruins of buildings and equipment mostly date from the 1930s when the May Lundy's tailings were reworked during the Great Depression.

Be extremely careful if you go off trail to explore the very steep, unstable slope above the lake. Long ago there was a well-defined trail to the upper works of the May Lundy Mine. Determined hikers will be rewarded with the remains of a tiered bunk/cookhouse clinging to the mountain, ore carts, tramway support towers and sundry mining artifacts. Besides mining history, the site, 1000 feet above Oneida Lake, offers wonderful views of Lake Canyon, Mount Warren and other peaks to the east.

Find your way above the lower, trailside tunnel and head toward the A-frames that once supported the tramway. As directed in Jim Hanna's book, *Lundy: Gem of the Eastern Sierra*, pick up a switchbacking path after 500 feet or so of rock scrambling. Follow it up to a point beneath the remains of the bunkhouse and continue uphill to the left until you reach the rock foundations of the former building. Please don't remove any souvenirs. Leave things in place for others to "discover." Due to the danger of cave-ins and bad air, tunnels in the area have been dynamited shut.

At 3.3 miles Crystal Creek flows out of the sealed lower mine tunnel, and rusted tram tracks run to the top of the mine's waste dump. See if you can discern the original shoreline of Crystal Lake before 60,000 to 70,000 tons of mine tailings partially filled it in. You'll pass more mining artifacts and junk before arriving at the willow-ringed shore of Oneida Lake, elevation 9600 feet. Looking at the abrupt rise of the Tioga Crest, it's almost unbelievable that a few men and mules schlepped eight tons of mining equipment over the

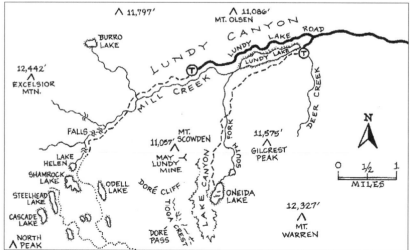

summit. Decades ago there was a trail above Ada Lake to Warren Canyon (see Chapter 10). Look sharp to find evidence of an old mining prospect on the rocky headwall above the little lake.

Although the trail is virtually covered by rock slides, hardy and experienced hikers can top Doré Pass and work their way down to Saddlebag Lake. Most, however, will choose to linger in 29-acre Oneida Lake's serene, subalpine environment. Before returning, consider an easy, half-mile junket to Ada Lake, unnamed on maps, at the canyon headwall. A use trail to the left of Oneida will get you there in a few minutes. Perfect peace and quiet rule the atmosphere in little Ada's rocky basin.

The hike through the main corridor of Lundy Canyon is less taxing. You'll find the trailhead two miles beyond the little resort at the end of the road. A busy beaver population has dammed lower Mill Creek in several places, creating sparkling shallow ponds and interesting Kodak moments. Lower Lundy Falls is an easy 0.6-mile walk, offering a stunning sample of the canyon's beauty that tempts you to go farther. Although not very high or wide, the rowdy cataract looks textured as it races over a rough, rocky surface. The water takes on an unusual, gleaming whiteness due to the darkness of underlying metamorphic rock. A short walk to the base of the falls gives another perspective of the playful cascade.

For more scenery that will leave you slack-jawed, continue to 1.5 miles where the path meanders through an extensive stand of huge aspens, complete with the remains of a roofless log cabin. Wildflowers are splendid along this stretch. Beyond the cabin, you'll marvel at nameless cascades streaming down the sheer canyon walls. Around 2.5 miles, look ahead for stair-stepping, slender Upper Lundy Falls plunging through a slot atop the canyon's near-vertical wall. If you choose to see the stupendous vista topside, it's that sheer wall you must tackle. If not, take time to enjoy this magnificent scene before returning to the trailhead.

Besides turning around when you approach the headwall, two other options are available to stalwart trail pounders. A grueling, steep, exposed hike to the top of Upper Lundy Falls on the Sierra Crest is incredibly scenic. You'll readily understand why so many canyon lovers deem Lundy the most beautiful in the Eastern Sierra. First, though, you must cautiously negotiate a series of switchbacks over a large, unstable talus slope. Rock slides have obliterated parts of the trail, and only occasionally is it rebuilt. About 1000 feet and half a million heartbeats later, you'll top the 10,000-foot-high crest. Just beyond the high point, you'll spot Lake Helen at 3 miles.

If you've arranged a shuttle, continue walking through Twenty Lakes Basin and its classic alpine scenery. This rewarding trans-Sierra trek, obviously, can start at Saddlebag Lake and end at Lundy Lake. Check the map for two routes that fork around Saddlebag and inquire at Saddlebag Lake Store and

Café about a boat taxi ride across, saving you two miles of walking. Hikers take note that the first third of the trip down to Lundy Trailhead, even though drop-dead gorgeous, is very hard on the knees and very airy if you have a problem with exposed heights.

However you choose to experience Lundy, the canyon's real gold remains available to all of us. The treasures of majestic mountains, cascading streams, vibrant wildflowers, sparkling lakes, lush aspen groves, placid beaver ponds, numerous waterfalls and astonishing fall color await your discovery.

Lake Helen sits near the top of Lundy Canyon.

10

Warren Canyon
Where Scenery and History Conspire

◆ THE DETAILS

Getting There: Drive 4.4 miles east from Tioga Pass, and park on the south side of Highway 120 near the 9000-foot elevation sign (the 9000 feet sign was missing at press time). The unmarked trail begins on the north side of the road behind a locked green gate. Or from Lee Vining, drive west on Highway 120 for about 9 miles to trailhead.

Nearest Campground: Tioga Lake or Ellery Lake, one and 2 miles respectively, east of Tioga Pass in Inyo National Forest, both open June through September. If those are full, you'll find 200 more sites for tents and RVs in several campgrounds farther east toward Lee Vining. Turn right (south) on Poole Power Plant Road to reach them. Except for Big Bend, all the camps are non-reservable.

Lodging/Services: Tioga Pass Resort, www.tiogapassresort.com, on Highway 120 near the intersection of Saddlebag Lake Road has housekeeping cabins, store, good café. Lee Vining on the shore of Mono Lake has several motels.

Further Info: Mono Basin Ranger Station, Inyo National Forest 760-647-3044.

User Groups: Hikers and horses. Dogs OK on leash. No mountain bikes.

Hike Distance: 6 miles round trip to the pass over Mount Warren's ridge.

Difficulty: Moderately strenuous.

Best Times to Go: After snowmelt, generally in early July, through October.

Elevation: 9000 feet at trailhead, 10,600 feet at pass.

Other Maps: USGS Mount Dana 7.5-minute topo, **Hoover Wilderness Map** for the big picture.

Cautions: Bighorn sheep habitat—no goats, dogs must be leashed or under voice control.

OF INTEREST
◆ Majestic alpine setting.
◆ Backdoor route to May Lundy Mine works.
◆ Little known trail.
◆ Nearby historic Bennettville site.
◆ Excellent food and lodging at nearby Tioga Pass Resort.

I've long been a fan of the resplendent scenery and excellent hiking and climbing routes in the Tioga Crest environs just east of Yosemite National Park. The landscape's robust beauty and solitude frequently draw me into its ancient embrace. Although hiking is often difficult in the alpine neighborhood above 10,000 feet, the rewards are completely worth negotiating steep trails in oxygen-scarce air. It's a region of high, bouldery meadows that look like enormous Zen gardens, icy lakes and tarns, flashing, flower-lined streams and sky-scraping peaks. The seeming closeness of the blue Sierra sky and staggering vistas produce top-of-the-world euphoria for those who choose to trek in timberline country.

Besides majestic scenery, if you wander in the Tioga Crest area long enough, you're likely to come across mining camp carcasses. Rusty pipes and machinery, altar-like mounds of tailings, huge stumps, dangerous open shafts and tunnels, mortarless stone foundations and rotting buildings remind us that we are not the first humans to set foot in this alpine world. Sometimes you'll discover snatches of faint or overgrown trails that either end abruptly or seem to go nowhere. The collusion of historical remnants and striking scenery is intriguing and often adds another layer of enjoyment and adventure to the outing.

Rarely visited Warren Canyon, on the edge of Hoover Wilderness within Inyo National Forest, contains these appealing components. My first foray into the gorge was prompted by tidbits of information from a retired Forest Service ranger. He talked about an ancient, mysterious and seemingly implausible trail connecting Lake Canyon to Warren Canyon via a shallow pass over Mount Warren's ridge. Even in the 1970s the trail was vague in places, but some beautifully constructed switchbacks up and over the rocky summit were still intact.

The mention of an obscure trail immediately piqued my curiosity. Then, comments about old pipes, cabin ruins, weathered beams and bleached-out, three-foot-high lodge pole stumps grabbed me like a Gila monster. I began scanning history books and maps, pestering Forest Service personnel and yakking with old timers familiar with the area. To date, no definite reason for the existence of either the trail or cabin has been documented. History books reveal no information, and an Inyo National Forest archaeologist can only offer an educated guess. Furthermore, the trail is not indicated on an 1893 USGS map.

However, we do know the Tioga Crest region is a repository of significant Sierra events brought about by the quest for precious metals. Today, though, few clues remain to verify the existence of what was known as the Great Silver Belt. Eclipsed at first by extraordinary gold and silver strikes at Bodie and Aurora to the northeast near the Nevada border, the Tioga Mining District wasn't organized until 1878. The following year miners in and around nearby Lundy Canyon formed the Homer Mining District.

*Early season in Warren Canyon
with Gilcrest Peak in the distance*

During the late nineteenth century, the clang and rumble of hard rock mining machinery and rowdy shouts of pack train handlers could be heard on either side of Tioga Crest. The excitement and energy were palpable as hundreds of men burrowed into the mountainsides in search of rich pay dirt. All of this frenzied activity took place before construction of the Great Sierra Wagon Road, predecessor of Highway 120, from the west in 1883.

A 56-mile-long road was built in only 130 days with just hand tools and dynamite which reached the mining camp and headquarters at Bennettville in the rugged alpine region of Tioga Hill. Previously, access was only possible over steep and treacherous trails. The journey to transport supplies and equipment by trail was so arduous and time-consuming that Great Sierra Consolidated Silver Company executives agreed to punch a road through the mountains to service the needs of their camps and transport ore to market.

The highly touted mining operation was short-lived and an utter failure. Not one ounce of silver was extracted, and the mines closed in 1884. It's doubtful the Great Sierra Wagon Road was ever used, and for the next 31 years the unmaintained road fell into serious disrepair. Eventually, in 1915, it was acquired by the federal government as a valuable tourist corridor through Yosemite National Park.

It's unlikely we'll ever know with certainty what the Warren Canyon Trail was all about or who built it. Nonetheless, it's conceivable that it was intended to schlep timber to Bodie to help satisfy the town's insatiable appetite for cordwood and mine timbers prior to 1879 when William Lundy operated a sawmill at Lundy Lake. As you will see, it assuredly would have been a formidable journey up and over the pass between Warren Canyon and Lake Canyon, but then that was an era filled with Herculean projects.

It also might have provided another connection from the Eastern Sierra to the rich May Lundy Mine in Lake Canyon, as well as access to Lundy town or Bennettville. Perhaps someone tried his luck at mining in the canyon. According to Jim Hanna, John Muir's great-grandson and author of *Lundy:*

Gem of the Eastern Sierra, the trail was the primary travel conduit between Lee Vining Canyon and Bennettville. Whatever the mostly vanished trail's purpose, actual or intended, the canyon was named by members of Whitney's geological survey for Kemble Warren, a figure in the Pacific Railroad surveys and a Civil War general.

Follow Highway 120 east from Tioga Pass for 3.6 miles to a major hairpin bend in the road below Ellery Lake. Watch for a 9000-foot elevation sign (missing at press time) on the right (south) side of the highway. In an area overlooking awesome Lee Vining Canyon, you'll find ample parking space in what climbers call Camp 9 or Camp 9K. However, the Forest Service no longer permits camping, and you run the risk of a citation if you spend the night. Pick up the unsigned trail directly across the highway behind a green metal gate. There is also room for two or three cars by the locked gate.

Begin walking on an abandoned road alongside Warren Creek, technically the Warren Fork of Lee Vining Creek. About a quarter-mile long, the road once accessed twelve primitive, pine-shaded campsites near the stream. Now the area is a quiet walk-in camp for canyon explorers and peak baggers. At road's end a sign announces that dogs must be under control and no goats are allowed past the lodge pole pine forest in Hoover Wilderness. I was puzzled by the reference to goats until I learned that they are sometimes used as pack animals. They are not allowed in Warren Canyon because it is bighorn sheep habitat. Domestic goats and sheep can transmit a fatal strain of pneumonia to the highly endangered wild sheep.

Do not expect to travel a clearly defined 2.5-mile-long trail to near the headwall as shown on the 1987 Hoover Wilderness map. For decades there hasn't been a continuous route to the pass, elevation 10,600 feet. There is no sign at the pass, and it is not marked on any map. An unmaintained use trail peters out in about 1.5 miles. Veteran hikers have learned that a map does not necessarily accurately show the territory. Some so-called updated maps are just carbon copies of their predecessors. Furthermore, neither the 1953 Mono Craters topo nor Inyo National Forest map show a trail. The 1994 7.5-minute Mount Dana topo, indicates a three-quarter-mile-long trail section that ends just inside the unsigned Hoover Wilderness boundary.

Unless you really work at it, you can't get lost in the three-mile-long canyon. If you're uncomfortable without the security of the path accurately represented on a map, you can always approximate the trail by following Warren Creek. As you climb higher, the end will be obvious when you see the solid rock headwall between you and Lake Canyon on the other side.

Beyond the sign the trail passes through a squishy meadow laced with little streams. These rills are present even in late October, given a year of normal precipitation. In July and August many species of wildflowers thrive in the spongy grassland. Please stay on the trail or, if it's too wet, skirt the meadow's east (right) side rather than blaze another route. Massive Tioga Peak juts skyward to the left and high above you. Soon, graceful, trembling aspens come into view. Resist the temptation to carve your initials on them as some thoughtless hikers have done. Pass a mostly dry meadow and reenter a lodge pole forest. A perky streamlet on the right about one-half mile from the campground sign indicates you've just entered Hoover Wilderness.

As the canyon steepens, keep right, staying to the edge of the trees where they come into contact with rocky slopes. Be on the lookout for old tree blazes hacked close to the ground. Their placement is odd because blazes are usually cut at eye level so they can easily be seen. Whoever cut these marks

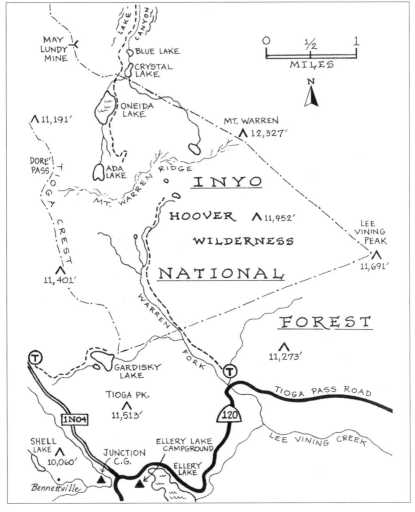

evidently didn't take snowfall into account, which would quickly bury them.

Higher still, stay on the right side of a steep, V-shaped gorge, and stay right again at a large, open meadow. The trail ends as you enter the huge grassy bowl. Ringed with peaks, it's a very photogenic place, especially in fall when the grass and willows glow with a soft golden light. Walk through lodge pole pine forest above a willow thicket on the meadow's right edge. If you're feeling a bit insecure at this point, don't fret. There really is no wrong way to walk up Warren Canyon. Keep going, stay right and ascend toward the lowest, most obvious pass over the headwall.

Watch for a little flat or clearing on your right as the canyon levels out a bit. You'll notice thigh-high, silvery stumps scattered throughout the area. Here you might stumble across the scanty remains of a hand-hewn cabin. A few lodge pole beams, corroded pipes and shallow trenches are all that's left to suggest human occupancy in the canyon. To date, there is no record of the cabin's builder or why it was constructed here. The stumps and trenches, however, hint at logging or prospecting. Please don't disturb the site or remove anything. Some day it may give up a clue about its history in this remote, rugged canyon.

Pick your way through granite outcrops and small boulders above the clearing and aim for the stark pass on the horizon just ahead. As you approach the head of the canyon, be sure to note the abrupt contact zone where brick-red metamorphic rocks meet grayish-white granite. Over the many years since the trail was built, numerous rock slides and avalanches have wiped out the skillfully constructed switchbacks leading to the saddle on Mount Warren's ridge. But, it is not that difficult to contour up the bare, rocky slope to the col and gape in wonder at stunning bird's-eye views of Warren Canyon and Lake Canyon. Unless storm clouds are gathering, take plenty of time to enjoy the timberline terrain.

To the east, Mount Warren's curved 12,327-foot summit beckons climbers. It's a Class 2 trip to the top where you'll find a register, helicopter pad and small radio repeater structure. Views of Mono Lake Basin, Mount Dana and a passel of other High Country peaks are fabulous. Although you can reach the peak from Lundy/Lake Canyons, there is less elevation gain and distance from the lower end of Warren Canyon.

When you must, return to the trailhead. Strong hikers with giddyup to spare should consider visiting Lake Canyon. Or, if you've planned ahead and arranged for a shuttle or someone to retrieve you, descend steeply into beautiful Lake Canyon, dotted with lakes and rich with mining history (see Chapter 9). Once in the canyon, follow the abandoned toll road past the workings of the famous May Lundy Mine down to Lundy Lake. The trail on the north side of Warren Ridge has also succumbed to slides. It's a strenuous haul up and over the pass, especially if you're toting a backpack. Be extra careful on the way down.

Hikers atop Mount Warren scan for bighorn sheep, with Mono Lake as a backdrop.

When I returned to the trailhead and looked at cars scooting up and down Highway 120, I figured out why Warren Canyon is blessedly empty. In most cases, it's a long and difficult trailhead approach that keeps crowds away. Although it's easy to get here, and Warren's entrance is barely off the road, the unsigned trailhead is hard to spot while winding through dramatically scenic Lee Vining Canyon. Motorists must pay attention on the steep, curvy grade or risk a quick trip to the bottom of the deep gorge's one-of-a-kind beauty. The green metal gate to the side of a sharp curve simply doesn't register much of a blip on the radar screen.

Glacier Canyon
High and Wild

◆ THE DETAILS

Getting There: From Lee Vining drive west on Highway 120/Tioga Road for 11 miles to Tioga Lake Overlook parking area on your left. The rest area has tables and vault toilets located about one mile east of Tioga Pass entrance station to Yosemite Park. You can see the trail from the parking area. Walk down the slope toward Tioga Lake's inlet stream to a wooden sign marked "Glacier Canyon-Dana Lakes." Mileage starts here. Note: At press time, the wooden sign was missing, although the post was still in place.

Nearest Campground: Tioga Lake (Inyo County) has 13 fee sites for tents and small RVs with fire grills, piped water, tables, toilets. Leashed pets OK. Open June through September. Non-reservable. Often windy in late afternoon.

Further Info and Permits: Inyo National Forest, Mono Basin Ranger Station 760-647-3044.

Lodging/Services: Nearby Tioga Pass Resort, www.tiogapassresort.com, has housekeeping cabins, a store and a good café. Lee Vining has Lake View Lodge 760-647-6543 and other motels.

User Groups: Hikers, no dogs because of bighorn sheep habitat.

Hike Distance: 5 miles round trip.

Difficulty: Moderately strenuous to Dana Lake; strenuous including Dana Plateau.

Elevation: 9700 feet at trailhead, 11,200 feet at Dana Lake.

Best Times to Go: Summer and fall.

Cautions: No dogs allowed. Avoid walking or camping in meadows. Backpacker limit is 5 people. If a storm is brewing, vacate the rocky setting in the upper canyon and/or Dana Plateau. NEVER take a thunderstorm for granted.

Other Maps: **Ansel Adams Wilderness** is best. USGS 7.5-minute topos Mount Dana and Tioga Pass.

OF INTEREST

◆ Fascinating hanging-glacial-valley geology.

◆ Wonderful alpine wildflowers.

◆ Bighorn sheep habitat.

◆ Easy access to the fabulous views from the Dana Plateau.

◆ Spectacular alpine scenery in the Tioga Pass environs.

◆ Nearby historic Bennettville site.

A moderate trail up Glacier Canyon guides you into an infrequently visited rocky realm just east of Yosemite Park's Tioga Pass. Solitude seekers will find the serenity and multifaceted beauty of this alpine environment much to their liking. The canyon is also seventh heaven for high elevation wildflower and geology enthusiasts. Glacier Canyon yields some of the most scenic hiking available anywhere in the Sierra Nevada. Few canyons offer such a mélange of natural features for only a modest investment of time and energy.

Although surrounded by acres of barren granite, the stream-cut valley floor is verdant and luxuriant with flowers. Music of snowmelt fills the air, downright therapy, Sierra-style, for High Country hikers. The 2.5-mile route to the headwall and the milky turquoise waters of Dana Lake will soon have you panting but not because it's wickedly steep. Starting high at 9700 feet and ascending to 11,200 feet is not something most of us do everyday. If you're unacclimated or a bit out of condition, pause often and absorb the canyon's stellar beauty.

At the west end of Tioga Lake, pick up the signed trail which winds through a lodge pole pine forest and shortly reaches Glacier Creek, unnamed on maps. Locals and climbers usually refer to it as Tioga Lake's inlet. In about 0.8 mile the path enters Ansel Adams Wilderness at 9800 feet and fords to the left side of the exuberant but narrow creek. Pockets of wildflowers flourish along the banks of the narrow, dashing stream on its way to Tioga Lake. The steepest section of the trail lies within the first mile. The incline abates beyond the unsigned wilderness boundary, and the terrain opens up as you enter the canyon itself.

The steep-walled canyon is aptly named. A long-vanished river of ice bulldozed the landscape as it crept through here en route to Mono Lake. Imagine the sight of icebergs floating on its then vast surface! The stunning gorge is technically a "hanging valley" created by a smaller tributary glacier. Hanging valleys are usually suspended high above the main glacial corridor. At the head of a side valley, such as Glacier Canyon, is a cirque where a glacier originated. A cirque, or glacial basin, typically contains a lake, below which sometimes is a chain of them, stair-stepping down-canyon like beads on a rosary.

As the grade eases and the landscape widens, watch for a creek descending a rocky gully on the left. It may be dry by fall, but its course is quite obvious. If you're feeling frisky and adventurous, follow the stream bed up gently sloping Dana Plateau. It's a nontechnical ascent onto an enormous, unglaciated, flat-topped plateau. Besides fabulous views from its 11,600-foot vantage point into Glacier Canyon and eastward toward Lee Vining, Mono Lake and Bodie Hills, look for the rare two-inch-tall snow willow.

Through hikers will continue straight ahead into an increasingly lush environment packed with wildflowers in late July and August, springtime at this elevation. As much as possible, avoid walking through the boggy grassland that stretches nearly to the headwall. It may not seem so, but these high meadows are very fragile ecosystems and home to myriad life forms. An old saying reminds us, "Alpine vegetation grows by the inch and dies by the foot."

The nearly level trail ceases to exist in the meadow. Don't fret about losing it because there's no place to go in the narrow valley except straight ahead. As

Dana Lake nestles beneath the canyon headwall at the top of Glacier Canyon.

you have been, keep to the left of the creek as you ramble up-canyon along the meadow's edge. Please don't trailblaze through the unsullied grassland. Damage to timberline vegetation takes decades to heal. Help keep it pristine and free of ugly ruts.

Ahead, the massive, truncated northeast face of Mount Dana, Yosemite's second tallest peak, completely dominates the horizon. Experienced mountaineers find its sheer wall an exhilarating climbing challenge. For the rest of us less vertical travelers, don't even think about it. The 13,053-foot mountain, plateau, lake, glacier and canyon were named in honor of James D. Dana (1813-1895), who is considered the foremost geologist of his era. The Yale professor provided the first comprehensive summary of North American geology.

At the top of the meadow, Glacier Creek disappears under tons of rock fall. The green wetland is replaced by stark, boulder-strewn terrain, and the contrast between the two land forms is abrupt and amazingly beautiful. It's delightful to hear the hidden creek's voice clinking merrily among the rocks beneath your boots. There is no trail through the talus field. Simply pick your route, stepping carefully on granite chunks, some the size of a microwave oven, some much larger.

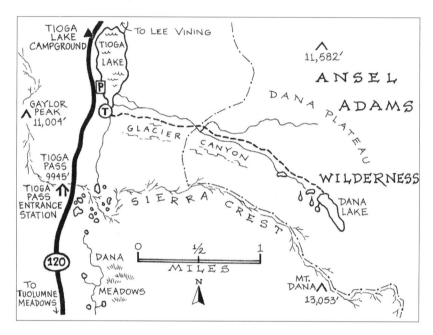

As you travel over the jumble of boulders, stop now and then to feast on the canyon's banquet of sights and sounds. You're near timberline in an awesome world of bright, naked stone. Yet, here and there, clusters of white columbine thrive in rocky crevices, a soft and lovely touch in the minimal-ist setting. Be aware that you are intimately experiencing a realm in nature unknown to the vast majority of humankind. To heighten the moment and indelibly imprint it in your heart, drink it in as if it were both the first and last time you will ever see this place.

When you reach the first small lake, I suggest walking around its right (west) side to negotiate the moraine above. Hie yourself up the 300-foot rocky slope and pass two more little lakes shortly before arriving at Dana Lake, elevation 11,200 feet. Last and largest in the series, one-third-mile-long Dana Lake hunkers directly below the sheer backside of Mount Dana. Set in a granite saucer, its unusual aqua hue is all the more remarkable because of the severe setting. The color is created by light reflecting off finely ground

Looking down upper Glacier Canyon, with Shepherd Crest and Excelsior Mountain in the distance

glacial debris suspended in the water. Swimmers beware. Brace yourself for a breath-robbing dip. This is, after all, a glacier-fed lake more than two miles above sea level.

Glacier Canyon is a designated bighorn sheep habitat, and if you're really lucky you may see one. Bighorns are hard to spot because they blend so perfectly into the landscape. Said one observer, "They look like rocks with legs." Regarded by John Muir as "the bravest of all mountaineers," they are one of the most endangered mammals in North America. A program to reestablish bighorn sheep in historic Sierra Nevada habitats and increase their numbers began in 1979. Widely scattered in little bands, there are only about 300 wild sheep left in the entire Sierra Nevada.

Clumps of stunted pine, tough-as-whipcord survivors of winter's rage, huddle around the shore. Only a few hundred years old, a glacier clings to the headwall amphitheater above the lake as a reminder of the great tongue of ice that once filled the canyon. It's one of a hundred or so small, shrunken remnants of the Sierra's former vast glacial system.

Although you're not far from Highway 120, you've walked into an uninhabited world away from civilization's distractions. Settle on a chunk of granite and enter the solitude of Glacier Canyon. Let it fill you with its powerful, yet peaceful, energy. Linger in the strangely beautiful landscape as long as you can before returning to Tioga Lake. You'll be treated to splendid vistas of the High Country above Tuolumne Meadows and Tioga Pass on the way back. If you bypassed it on the way in and still have some zip in your legs, scramble up Dana Plateau before leaving the canyon. The views are utterly astounding.

12

Gibbs Canyon
Serenity Beneath Yosemite Park's Eastern Rim

◆ THE DETAILS

Getting There: From Lee Vining, drive south on Highway 395 for 1.2 miles from the Highway 120 intersection. Turn west and look for a small sign pointing the way to Horse Meadow. Ignore any side roads and proceed straight up the canyon. Continue for 3.2 miles to the primitive parking area and trailhead at the top end of Upper Horse Meadow. Beyond Lower Horse Meadow, a short, steep grade might require four-wheel drive. Park off road and walk a few minutes to the trailhead if you need to.

Nearest Campground: Lee Vining Creek, 3 miles west of Lee Vining on Highway 120/Tioga Pass Road. Turn left at the signed campground entrance on Poole Power Plant Road. There are 200 sites in several campgrounds strung out along Lee Vining Creek. All charge a fee and have tables, fire rings, pit toilets, but no drinking water. Dogs on leash OK. Open May to October. No reservations.

Lodging/Services: Lee Vining is a full-service small town overlooking Mono Lake. Try Lake View Lodge 760-647-6543 or Murphey's Motel 760-647-6316.

Further Info: Mono Lake Committee Information Center 760-647-6595 in Lee Vining, or Mono Basin Visitor Center 760-647-3044, one mile north of town.

User Groups: Hikers and horses. Dogs OK on leash. No mountain bikes.

Hike Distance: 6 miles round trip to Gibbs Lake, 7.5 miles round trip to Kidney Lake.

Difficulty: Moderately strenuous to Gibbs Lake, strenuous to Kidney Lake.

Best Times to Go: Summer and fall.

Elevation: 7960 feet at start, 9530 feet at Gibbs Lake, 10,388 feet at Kidney Lake.

Other Maps: **Ansel Adams Wilderness** is best, USGS 7.5-minute Mount Dana topo.

Cautions: Backpacking permits are available at Mono Basin Visitor Center. No fires at Kidney Lake. Spare the trees at Gibbs Lake and use a stove. Dead or alive, trees are part of the landscape and provide food and shelter for small animals and organic material to the soil. Wild sheep habitat—dogs must be leashed. Stay far away and don't appear threatening in any way.

Winter Sports: Road may be open and passable in winter, providing opportunities for cross-country skiing and snowshoeing. Also, cross-country skiing and snowshoeing around Mono Lake can be wonderful.

OF INTEREST
◆ Two pristine alpine lakes.

◆ Dramatic vistas of Mono Basin and the Eastern Sierra.
◆ Historic Basque-carved arborglyphs.
◆ Near Mono Lake for kayaking, canoeing and world-class birding.

Sometimes unsigned roads are a good thing. Focused on a preset destination, most travelers are reluctant to leave the familiarity and ease of a highway to venture into terra incognita. They'll probably never experience the adventure and serendipity inherent in following the road less traveled. But, for those of us keen on getting away from the crowd, their loss is our gain. There's a lot of lonely territory out there awaiting exploration by those who've been bitten by the back road bug.

One such unmarked road is an easily missed turnoff to Horse Meadow, 1.2 miles south of the Highway 395/120 junction in Lee Vining. The dusty byway skirts the edge of Lower and Upper Horse Meadow, verdant and blessed with a sea of lavender wild iris in early summer, en route to Gibbs Lake Trailhead. Even if it were signed, I dare say only a handful of vacationers would be tempted to see where it leads. Only a few might be lured into the empty, sage-filled high desert landscape beyond the end of pavement.

However, connoisseurs of Eastern Sierra canyons know these uninviting dirt tracks invariably pass through gorgeous valleys on the way to camp-grounds or to trailheads that access wildly dramatic High Country scenery. They know the real wonders and personality of the range are revealed by entering these great troughs carved by ice and fine-tuned by water. Thanks to these roads, often bumpy and narrow, even non-hikers can enjoy the Sierra's majesty in ways freeway cruisers will never experience.

For hikers, the primary reason for driving into Horse Meadow is to reach little-known Gibbs Lake, an emerald green jewel at 9530 feet in Ansel Adams Wilderness within Inyo National Forest. It's set in a deep bowl at the base of Mount Gibbs and Mount Dana, 12,764 feet and 13,053 feet respectively. While in the neighborhood, energetic trekkers will want to cross-country 800 feet up to alpine Kidney Lake for spectacular views. The canyon, lake, creek and mountain were named for Oliver W. Gibbs (1822-1908), professor of science at Harvard.

After veering from Highway 395, the road immediately forks. Proceed straight ahead through Indian land, and look sharp on the right for a small wooden sign, "Horse Meadow, one mile," nearly obscured by a clump of sage. The Matleys, a Mono Basin pioneer family, once ranched in the area and grazed cattle and sheep. The canyon was arid and covered with sage until they diverted Gibbs Creek water. Evidence of shallow ditches is extant in the meadow.

Avoid any turnoffs as you drive to Lower Horse Meadow. Piñon pines are common along the lower roadway. Their tasty, nutritious nuts were an important staple in the diet of local Indians. Ordinary passenger cars should not have trouble negotiating the road for the first 2.3 miles. Beyond that there is a short, steep grade best suited for four-wheel drive or high-clearance vehicles. There is a pullout just before the steep pitch if you need to park and walk. The eastern end of Upper Horse Meadow is only 200 feet ahead.

After the incline, the road levels out to the heavily forested trailhead, 3.2 miles from the highway. Many old aspens live around the meadow and next to the stream. Long ago, Basque shepherds etched their names and images on some of them. They represent a valuable historic resource. Please do not deface them or add your own message. The meadow is bordered on the north by the enormous right flank of Lee Vining Canyon's lateral moraine. Ahead to the west looms the formidable wall of Dana Plateau and Mount Dana.

The road splits as you near the end. Either direction will soon lead to the small parking area. The trail begins at 7960 feet behind a locked gate and climbs sharply for a mile on a very rough road. Occasionally, the Los Angeles Department of Water and Power uses it to check on water diversion locks upstream. At a little dip in the road, take a breather and look back for a fine view of sapphire blue Mono Lake. While trudging uphill through the mixed forest, note the many species of wildflowers cheering you on. Farther up, turn around and take in Horse Meadow, Mono Craters, Aeolian Buttes and the mystical White Mountains shimmering in the distance.

Around .75 mile, the grade briefly flattens and then drops to dashing Gibbs Creek. This is a pleasant spot for a snack break. The road climbs again and forks after passing over a flume pipe. To the right are the diversion locks, but

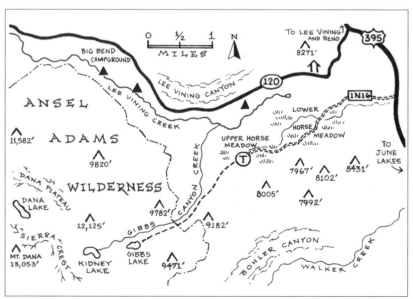

Gibbs Lake is dwarfed by Mount Gibbs.

you'll bear left and soon leave the road behind. Now on a single track, ascend and cross a ridge above Gibbs Canyon Creek. After climbing a dry ravine, the path levels out on a flower-studded shoulder above the stream. It's here that you begin to sense the alpine world you're about to enter. The skyline is filled with the imposing presences of Mount Gibbs and Mount Dana aligned along the eastern edge of Yosemite National Park.

At 2.3 miles a sign marks the Ansel Adams Wilderness boundary near the racing creek, lush with a host of wildflowers. Currant, Labrador tea, red heather, mountain laurel and thickets of fragrant azalea prosper in the beautiful riparian environment. Most of the elevation gain is now over except for a short stint to the outlet of Gibbs Lake at 3 miles and 9530 feet elevation.

Rimmed by whitebark pine and mountain hemlock, glittering Gibbs Lake more than compensates for the 1600-foot climb. Use trails lead left and right; take one and settle in for lunch, perhaps a nap or a swim. Aside from a seagull or two up from Mono Lake, you'll most likely have this corner of the Eastern Sierra all to yourself. Backpackers will find fair to good campsites south (left) of the outlet.

On the far side, the outlet of Kidney Lake spills down a rocky slope, and the solitude is so deep that you can hear it cascading into the lake. Be sure to visit Kidney Lake after you're rested. Although there is no official trail, you'll have no difficulty finding the route. When you're ready, follow the south side of the inlet stream for about 0.75 mile to the upper lake, 800 feet above. Absolute serenity and expansive views are worth the steep jaunt.

As alpine ponds go, 1250-foot-long Kidney Lake is quite large, almost twice the size of Gibbs. Named for its kidney-shaped outline, the 10,388-

foot jewel sits in a barren talus basin on the brink of timberline beneath Mount Dana. Most of the shoreline is stark and treeless, save for a clutch of gnarled whitebark pines at the eastern end. Backpackers can find meager shelter among them from the fierce wind that often screams over the crest. A few more protected sites can be found below the lake near the creek. Practice zero impact camping and remember that no fires are permitted at this elevation.

Retrace your steps when it's time to leave. On the way back, spectacular, almost surreal, views of Mono Basin will rivet your attention. It's a landscape shaped by both ancient and recent volcanic forces. Landlocked Mono Lake is at least 730,000 years old and covers 70 square miles. Mono's two islands, Pahoa and Negit, rose violently from the lake within the last 1700 years. Before diversion of its Sierran tributary streams began in 1941 by the Los Angeles Department of Water and Power, the lake was much larger and much less saline. At maximum size the ice-age inland sea spread across 338 square miles and was five times larger and six times deeper than the modern lake.

To the south are the symmetrical Mono Craters, a ten-mile-long range of sleeping volcanoes. They've been called the youngest mountains in North America. Although their history reaches back 40,000 years, Panum Crater was formed just 630 years ago. Named for the Roman god of wind, the weathered Aeolian Buttes are the oldest formation in Mono Basin, dating back about 750,000 years. On the far horizon are the beautiful White Mountains, home to California's third tallest peak. White Mountain is only 250 feet lower than Mount Whitney.

Wooded slopes surround Gibbs Lake.

Sheep are no longer allowed in Horse Meadow because of possible contact with wild bighorn sheep. Domestic sheep carry a strain of pneumonia that is fatal to bighorns. Wild sheep are one of the most endangered mammals in North America, rarer than the Florida panther or California condor. They are the quintessential symbol of High Sierra wilderness, reminding us of an era when their mountain realm was vastly less accessible and altered by modern humans. Hanging on in dispersed little bands, only about 300 of these magnificent monarchs of High Country remain in the entire Sierra Nevada. A sighting of Elvis above timberline is more likely than catching a glimpse of a bighorn sheep. Sightings are exceedingly rare, but if you do see them, stay far away. Your presence may negatively impact their behavior and scare them to higher ground where sparse forage and severe climatic conditions could affect their survival.

Hikes in the Eastern Sierra, such as the journey into the heart of Gibbs Canyon, always remind me of John Muir's wisdom, eloquence and love for his "range of light." Perhaps your soul will resonate with one of his poignant observations. "Oh, these vast, calm, measureless mountain days . . . in whose light everything seems divine . . . nevermore, however weary, should one faint by the way who gains the blessing of one mountain day. Whatever his fate, short life, long life, stormy or calm, he is rich forever."

13

Bloody Canyon
An Ancient Transmontane Corridor

◆ THE DETAILS

Getting There: From Lee Vining, drive south on US Highway 395 for 5 miles and turn right on Highway 158/June Lake Loop Road. Drive 1.5 miles and turn right onto Parker Lake Road. Follow it for .5 mile until it crosses a wide graded road, called the aqueduct road. Turn right and continue on the aqueduct road for nearly one mile, then turn left and drive 2 miles up a bumpy road to its end and a parking area at the base of a moraine at Walker Lake Trailhead.

NOTE: There are two trailheads for Walker Lake/Bloody Canyon. You want the more southerly of the two, NOT the one along Walker Creek. Although it is an alternative, it adds 2.5 miles in each direction.

Another option is a trans-Sierra crossing, requiring a car shuttle. Park one car at Mono Pass Trailhead in Yosemite Park at road marker T37 on Highway 120 and another at the recommended trailhead. This, too, is an extremely scenic route, demanding only a 900-foot gain in 4 miles to the pass. If you prefer less climbing, in this case much less climbing, begin the trans-Sierra trek through Bloody Canyon at Mono Pass Trailhead.

Nearest Campgrounds: Primitive, dry camping with fire rings and vault toilets is available at the trailhead. Lee Vining Canyon has 60 sites for tents and RVs in four separate campgrounds in Lower Lee Vining Canyon. In Upper Lee Vining Canyon are 73 sites along the creek in two adjacent campgrounds. Fee, no reservation, dogs on leash OK.

Lodging: Lee Vining has several, including Lake View Lodge 760-647-6543 and Murphey's Motel 760-647-6316.

Further Info: Mono Basin Ranger Station, Inyo National Forest 760-647-3044.

User Groups: Hikers. Dogs OK on leash east of Mono Pass only. No mountain bikes.

Hike Distance: 12 miles round trip.

Difficulty: Very strenuous.

Best Times to Go: Summer and autumn.

Cautions: Do not remove historic artifacts. Backpackers take note that there is virtually no level spot to camp in Bloody Canyon except for a small area by Upper Sardine Lake; Inyo National Forest permit required. No dogs allowed from Mono Pass west—Yosemite National Park. There is also no camping in the Mono Pass area inside Yosemite National Park. No dogs from Mono Pass west.

Elevation: 8200 feet at trailhead. Walker Lake, 7890 feet; Mono Pass, 10,600 feet.
Other Maps: USGS 7.5-minute Koip Peak topo or *Ansel Adams Wilderness.*

OF INTEREST

◆ Excellent geology accentuated by multicolored rocks and peaks.
◆ Rugged gateway to Yosemite Park backcountry.
◆ Abundant historic artifacts at Mono Pass.

Chatter marks on granite carved by a glacier

A few miles southwest of Mono Lake is the gateway to Bloody Canyon, one of the Eastern Sierra's most scenic glacier-carved canyons. It's also the location of an ancient trans-Sierra trade route established 9600 years ago by Native Americans, later used by miners in the 1800s. The canyon's sinister name is derived from the blood of pack animals cut by jagged rocks as they struggled through the narrow, treacherous gorge.

Many Eastern Sierra canyons are notorious for long, killer inclines that access pristine alpine locations. The Bloody Canyon Trail is definitely in that fraternity of grueling hikes. The six-mile trek to 10,600-foot Mono Pass straddling the Inyo National Forest and Yosemite National Park boundary travels through stunning, wild terrain. Because of its steepness and distance, day hikers and backpackers are a rare commodity. If you're out of shape and/ or unacclimated, the climb is a real wheezer.

Although challenging, especially if toting more than a day pack, the journey is well worth the heavy breathing involved in the 2700-foot ascent to the pass. If you're thinking it'll be easier on the way back, think again. The relentless downhill stress on knees and thighs will remind you that the gradient is severe in either direction.

Besides a trail less traveled, Bloody Canyon's rocky grandeur offers a clinic in High Country geology and an artist's palette of colors. From pale lavender-gray to the iron-rich, rusty red metamorphic rock formations, the canyon is alive with colors you'd not expect to see on naked stone. The sheen of glacial polish abounds, as do "chatter" marks, crescent-shaped gouges made by ice pressure. Near the trailhead, graceful lateral moraines cradle the azure waters of Walker Lake.

Looking west up Bloody Canyon, Walker Lake in the foreground

Only a few yards from the car, the trail immediately starts climbing with a .25-mile push to the top of a ridge. It then plunges 500 rocky feet in .75 mile to Walker Lake. But first, take a moment to gaze at the lovely, tree-ringed lake, named for a rancher, not the famous explorer. Aspen trees line the western shore, some of which bear the names and "artwork" of long-gone Basque shepherds.

A small dock and a few cabins mark an area of private property. On your way down, try to keep from grumbling about the struggle up this rough path at the end of a long day. Cross the inlet, and turn left (west) for Sardine Lakes and Mono Pass.

Relish a brief, rather level stretch before the trail begins an inexorable, but exquisitely scenic, ascent to the pass. At a sign announcing entry to Ansel Adams Wilderness around 1.5 miles, the trail begins switchbacking steeply alongside musical Walker Creek. When you pause for a breather, turn around for a superb down-canyon view of mile-long Walker Lake with Mono Lake shimmering in the distant flatlands.

Continue climbing beside the creek that begins life at the pass and ends at Mono Lake, a 3000-foot tumble of silvery snowmelt through the gash known as Bloody Canyon. In late July and early August, the wooded slopes are riotous with wildflowers. After crossing the creek on a log bridge, resume a steady ascent across a rocky bench.

The grade increases sharply as it switchbacks toward Lower Sardine Lake. At the top of a minor ridge, enjoy a wee break in the climb before negotiating more fatiguing zigzags. Take heart in knowing that the lake is just above the cascade flowing over huge rock slabs. A final, brief effort brings you to the edge of 9890-foot Lower Sardine Lake, a little more than 4 miles from the trailhead.

Take a long break and revel in the gorgeous alpine setting. Deep and cold, glittering with harsh beauty, the lake occupies a glacial bowl imprisoned by towering, barren cliffs. A brilliant wildflower display along the shore and

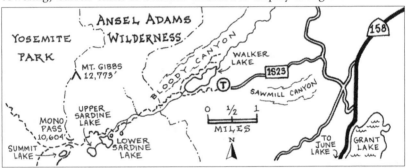

outlet creek softens the Spartan environment. The main event here is the absolutely knockout vista toward Mono Lake, certainly one you'll never forget.

Perhaps you're wondering why two Sierra lakes were named for a saltwater fish. According to local lore, an ill-fated mule bearing a heavy cargo of canned sardines to a mining camp fell off the trail and cartwheeled spectacularly before vanishing in the icy waters. Although the trail is safer now, hikers need to be mindful of their footing, particularly on tight switchbacks and loose talus. This is a rugged mountain trail, not one of the manicured, over-engineered "freeways" found in some Sierra locations. Truth is, many of us Sierra stompers enjoy an outing on a real trail because it heightens the adventure.

Marshal your energy for the remaining 1.5 miles to the pass, the steepest part of the hike. You'll notice from here on the canyon is actually more of a gorge as the walls close in and rise even more precipitously. It's not hard to understand how Bloody Canyon earned its name. Imagine tired, heavily bur-

Looking down Bloody Canyon from Upper Sardine Lake, with Mono Lake in the distance

dened pack animals being driven through this dangerously steep defile lined with splintery rocks.

In 1864 William Brewer of Whitney's California Geological Survey descended it and wrote, "You would pronounce it utterly inaccessible to horses, yet pack trains come up and down, but the bones of several horses and mules and the stench of others told that all had not passed safely. The trail comes down 3000 feet in less than four miles, over rocks and loose stones and over precipices. It was a bold man who first took a horse up there. The horses were so cut by sharp rocks they named it Bloody Canyon—and it's appropriate. Part of the way the rocks are literally sprinkled with blood from the animals."

There is a big change in elevation between Upper and Lower Sardine Lakes, requiring an arduous .75-mile climb. At its closest, the trail comes within .2 mile of Upper Sardine Lake where a backpacker can find a few small campsites nearby. The grade for the last .6 mile to Mono Pass mellows somewhat. The strenuous hike concludes at the "Mono Pass, el. 10600 ft." metal sign.

The pass environs are blessed with high visual drama and a rich cultural heritage reaching back to prehistoric times. The Bloody Canyon-Mono Pass Trail was a major transmontane corridor between the Ahwahneechees of Yosemite Valley and Northern Paiutes in Mono Lake Basin until about 1900. By then their annual rendezvous in Tuolumne Meadows had ended because there were so few Yosemite Indians left who had survived contact with the outside world. Present-day Tioga Road, formerly the Great Sierra Wagon Road, approximately follows a large portion of the ancient trail west of Tioga Pass.

News of a gold discovery in the area triggered a rush of prospectors to the Sierra Crest. Between 1852 and about 1890, hordes of miners worked claims on either side of the summit. To the southeast of tiny Summit Lake, a short trail leads to the ruins of cabins that housed workers of the Golden Crown and Ella Bloss Mines. It's worth the five-minute walk to inspect them at close range.

As you look out a cabin window opening be aware that where you've walked today keeps alive 96 centuries of human activity in this spectacular Sierra niche. You have commingled your footsteps with thousands of others who traveled the same path. You, too, are now part of the history of Bloody Canyon and Mono Pass.

June Lakes Basin and Parker Canyon
A Treasure Trove of Natural Beauty

◆ THE DETAILS

Getting There: From Lee Vining, drive 5 miles south on U.S. Highway 395, then turn right onto State Highway 158, June Lakes Loop Road. Go 1.5 miles, then turn right onto Parker Lake Road which heads directly toward the mountains for 2.5 miles to end at Parker Lake Trailhead. No water or toilets.

Since Highway 158 is a loop road, you can turn west on either end. The scenic byway skirts four lakes and passes through June Lake village on its 16-mile journey through the Basin before returning to Highway 395. Snowfall closes the loop's northern section in winter, but the southern end usually stays open.

Nearest Campgrounds: June Lakes Loop has seven campgrounds, mostly on the south end. Close to the hike is Silver Lake Campground with 65 sites and piped water, open May through September.

Lodging/Services: Historic Silver Lake Resort 760-648-7525 has housekeeping cabins and an excellent café. Boulder Lodge 760-648-7533 has cabins and motel units. If you plan to stay overnight, make reservations well in advance. An alternative is to stay in Lee Vining.

Further Info: June Lake Chamber of Commerce, P.O. Box 2, June Lake, CA 93529.

User Groups: Hikers and equestrians. Dogs OK on leash.

Hike Distance: 4 miles round trip to Parker Lake, 7 miles one way shuttle hike to Silver Lake.

Elevation: 8000 feet at trailhead. 400-foot gain to Parker Lake.

Difficulty: Moderate; moderately strenuous to Silver Lake.

Best Times to Go: Summer, autumn.

Cautions: No mountain bikes permitted.

Other Maps: USFS **Ansel Adams Wilderness** for both detail and an overview; USGS Koip Peak 7.5-minute topo.

OF INTEREST

- ◆ Moderate trail to a gorgeous alpine lake.
- ◆ Dramatic remnants of glacial activity.
- ◆ Grand vistas if you choose a shuttle hike to Silver Lake.

Hidden from motorists whizzing along Highway 395 near Lee Vining, four large lakes lie out of sight in June Lakes Basin. Like precious jewels, Grant, Silver, Gull and June Lakes gleam against the bases of colossal granite ramparts. They rest in a broad and uniquely formed horseshoe-shaped canyon, compliments of 24-square-mile Rush Creek Glacier. One of the numerous and luxuriant chasms in a sere and seemingly drab landscape, the one-of-a-kind, curved canyon drained by Rush Creek reveals itself quickly once you turn onto Highway 158, known as June Lakes Loop Road. The paved byway weaves through the Basin's grandeur in a 16-mile loop, winding spectacularly past the lakes before rejoining Highway 395.

Although an all-year resort concentrated around June Lake, the Basin's atmosphere is tranquil and relaxed, especially in comparison to its nearby neighbor, Mammoth Lakes. Cozied up at the base of sky-kissing Carson Peak and June Mountain, the resort area has a friendly, easygoing European charm. Attractive inns, motels and eateries cater to a wide range of budgets and tastes.

The loop is well known for its outstanding outdoor opportunities. June Mountain Ski Area is a popular destination for alpine and Nordic enthusiasts. In summer and autumn the June Lakes loop is a recreation paradise. Hiking, camping, cycling, sailing, fishing, horseback riding, photography, botanizing and water skiing (Grant Lake only) lure outdoor fans to this dramatic setting. Because of the soaring topography all around you, all the trails into the backcountry, except one, are steep and strenuous.

Early autumn in the Basin will hurl you into sensory overload. Quaking aspen groves set the slopes on fire with scarlet, burnished orange and brilliant gold, providing one of the most vivid fall pageants on Eastern Sierra mountainsides. Being in the midst of these fluttering, flamboyant trees is utterly memorable. Besides the garish aspen display, willows and cottonwoods lend their mellow, amber light to the show.

Human history in June Lakes is very old. The Numu (Paiute) people inhabited the area for millennia prior to the advent of miners and settlers. Mining, however, in the Basin itself amounted to only a flash in the pan. From the earliest days of its discovery by non-natives, the scenic loop was destined to become a lodestar for visitors enchanted by the natural world. Trouble in paradise surfaced early in the twentieth century when its abundant water resources caught the attention of developers in southern California. In 1917 the Rush Creek Powerhouse, first in a long and complicated series of water and land exploitations, was completed to slake the thirst of an exploding Los Angeles population.

During 1917 rustic Carson Camp, the region's pioneer tourist facility, was in business. Later the name was changed to Silver Lake Resort. In 1921, a rough dirt road from the main highway, a "wannabe" road in reality, was finished, allowing automobile access to the entire loop. Because of the new road, civilization

Parker Lake and it's headwall

poured in. The increase in permanent residents created a need for a post office, established in 1924. For years, mail was delivered by dog sled. The Basin glittered for a time as a playground for the rich and famous when Hollywood discovered the wildly picturesque locale and shot many movies at Silver and June Lakes.

Significant contributions to further development resulted from numerous Los Angeles water/power projects between 1920 and 1945 and the formation of June Lakes Winter Sports Association. Another boon to the Basin's growth occurred in 1961 when the first June Mountain ski lift opened, creating a winter industry that transformed the canyon into a year-round resort center. Over the subsequent decades, more accommodations and services were built for visitors who came to stay and play in this spectacular Eastern Sierra locale. So far, though, the village has maintained its quaintness and friendly, peaceful ambiance.

◆ THE HIKE

But for one, trails out of the Basin are vertical and strenuous. The exception is the 2-mile route to Parker Lake, a mere 400-foot gain in elevation from your car. The 24-acre lake is situated at the head of Parker Canyon, a side canyon at the extreme northern end of June Lakes Basin. The short cleft's architect was a glacier that overrode the crest in ancient, prehistoric times. A vestige of it is extant below 12,800-foot Koip Peak, headwaters for Parker Lake and Creek. A few other landmarks are also named for an early settler

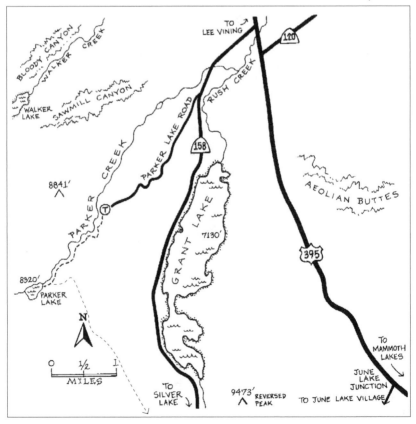

along the stream.

The 8000-foot trailhead is at the end of a 2.5-mile dirt spur off the June Lakes Loop Road near huge Grant Lake. The trail immediately climbs a moderate slope covered with the Eastern Sierra's signature plant species: sagebrush, piñon pine, rabbit brush, bitterbrush and feathery mountain mahogany. Most of the hike's elevation greets you in the first .75 mile as you ascend the back side of an intact terminal (front) moraine, a gargantuan mound of material bulldozed down-canyon by a glacier on the move. This moraine is unique because it's the only one in the region that looks like it did thousands of years ago, unbreached by streams and washouts.

As you make your way up the sandy moraine, turn around and gaze at Mono Lake, a bright blue eye shimmering on the desert floor. A map will help identify other features in your line of sight. As you near vigorous Parker Creek, typical high desert vegetation gives way to aspen thickets, little grassy meadows and stands of impressive Jeffrey and lodge pole pines. Somewhere along here, take a creekside break and listen to the music of snowmelt. Wildflowers increase in abundance as you get closer to the lake. The now forested trail closely follows the stream, passing a south-trending path to Silver Lake about one-half mile before arriving at Parker Lake. The serene setting paints a classic High Sierra picture.

Parker's dark green waters are hemmed in by lateral moraines and abruptly backdropped by colorful, soaring peaks. Above the head of the lake, a long waterfall spills down from Koip Peak over barren rock before fanning out to leap over a precipice. On a wind-calm day, you're gifted with another view of

Parker Lake nestles at the base of monumental Sierra peaks.

the 12,000-foot peaks above as they are reflected in the lake's pristine water.

Before leaving, you can explore the far end of the lake on a rough fishermen's trail on the south side. You'll enter an aspen grove at the head of the lake. Turn around here or bushwhack through willows and clamber over boulders around Parker's north shore until you regain the official trail back to your vehicle.

Prepared with sufficient energy, water, food and a shuttle car, you can extend your trek by veering right at the trail junction you passed on the way in. It leads to a trailhead at gorgeous Silver Lake, at 7200 feet elevation, in approximately 5 miles. This hike is much more enjoyable during the cooler days of late spring or early autumn because much of the little-used route travels across an exposed, sun-drenched, sagebrushy ridge. Its high point en route to the trailhead is 9200 feet. The trail's most and probably only redeeming feature is the heart-throbbing views of the surrounding terrain. Smashing vistas east to Mono Craters and Mono Lake, Silver Lake and the colony of majestic mountains encircling the Basin are definitely worth the extra mileage.

15
Fern and Yost Lakes
Short, Sweet and Steep

◆ THE DETAILS

Getting There: From Lee Vining, drive south on Highway 395 for 11 miles to the second June Lakes junction. Turn right on Highway 158, June Lakes Road, and drive through the picturesque village backdropped by classic sky-kissing Sierra peaks. Continue 1.3 miles past June Mountain Ski Area parking area, and watch for a hard-to-spot dirt road on your left, signed for Fern Creek. Turn in and park at the end. The trail begins behind a line of boulders.

Nearest Campgrounds: June Lakes Loop has seven campgrounds, mostly on the south end. Close to the hike is Silver Lake Campground with 65 fee sites and piped water.

Lodging/Services: Silver Lake Resort 760-648-7525 has housekeeping cabins, small store and an excellent café. Boulder Lodge 760-648-7533 has cabins and motel units. Make reservations well in advance. An alternative is to stay in Lee Vining.

Further Info: June Lake Chamber of Commerce, P.O. Box 2, June Lake, CA 93529. Inyo National Forest Supervisor's Office 760-873-2400.

User Groups: Hikers. Dogs OK on leash. No mountain bikes.

Hike Distances: (all round trip) From Fern Creek Trailhead to Fern Lake, 3.4 miles; Yost Lake, 4.8 miles; both lakes, 7.6 miles. One way shuttle hike to Glass Creek Trailhead, about 9 miles.

Difficulty: Strenuous to the lakes, very strenuous to Glass Creek Trailhead.

Best Times to Go: Summer for brilliant wildflower show in the meadows, autumn for fall color.

Cautions: Know how to read a map and have off-trail experience if Glass Creek Meadow is your destination.

Elevation: Fern Creek Trailhead, 7340 feet. Gain to Fern Lake is 1500 feet. Gain to Yost Lake is 1750 feet.

Other Maps: USFS ***Ansel Adams Wilderness*** or Tom Harrison's ***Mammoth High Country Trail Map***. Note: The trail between Yost Meadow and Glass Creek Meadow shown on the ***Ansel Adams Wilderness Map*** does not exist.

Winter Sports: Highway 158/June Lakes Loop Road is plowed in winter on the south end through the village as far as June Mountain Ski Area. Alpine and nordic skiing, snowshoeing, snowboarding, ice climbing and snow play are available in this enchanting canyon.

OF INTEREST
◆ Pretty lakes with a sublime alpine backdrop.
◆ Stunning views of June Lakes Basin.
◆ Peak-bagging and cross-country options for experience hikers.

Originally called Horseshoe Canyon because of its atypical, curved configuration, June Lakes Basin is one of the crown jewels in John Muir's "Range of Light." Not far from the sagebrush and monochromatic tones of the high

desert, the June Lakes landscape is another surprisingly colorful, luxuriant Eastern Sierra canyon. State Highway 158 meanders through the heart of the spectacularly scenic Basin on a 16-mile loop before rejoining Highway 395. A charming and relatively small resort village centered near June Lake hugs the bases of massive Carson Peak and June Mountain. June Lakes Loop is renowned for its superb and plentiful year-round recreational venues. From skiing to sailing to hiking, visitors will find a smorgasbord of outdoor activities in this dramatic setting.

Majestic Sierra junipers add flavor to many Eastern Sierra trails.

Towering peaks embrace the Basin, leaving no doubt that trails into the backcountry are steep and strenuous. The neighborhood is vertical, but it's worth every effort it takes to huff and puff to your destination. Although the paths to Fern and Yost lakes are short, don't expect them to be easy. You'll ascend relentlessly on what seems to be an interminable number of switchbacks to reach Fern's north shore, 1500 feet and 1.7 miles above the trailhead. Yost Lake requires a 1750-foot elevation gain in 2.4 miles.

I recommend visiting both lakes while in this neck of the woods, but if you have to choose just one, head for Fern Lake. This guide will direct you to each of them and also point the way to Glass Creek Meadow, via an easy cross-country ramble from Yost Lake. If you're in for the long haul to one of the largest meadows in the Eastern Sierra, you'll need to position a shuttle car or have someone pick you up (see Chapter 16).

FERN LAKE

From Fern Creek Trailhead at 7340 feet, a rocky path immediately climbs a steep, forested hill. Wheeze your way upward through a beautiful swath of large aspens. Wildflowers will cheer you on, as will over-the-shoulder-views of the southern half of June Lakes Basin, Reversed Peak and Mono Craters as you gain elevation. Flowers and vistas are always good reasons to pause and give your lungs a break. Enjoy cameo appearances of Carson Peak's sheer granite face through the dense forest cover.

Continue climbing among aromatic Jeffrey pines and stout Sierra junipers as the trail cuts left across a very steep slope at the half-mile mark. Take it easy along here because the path is narrow and the mountainside is severe. Note rugged Carson Peak, elevation 10,909 feet, to the right. The water music you hear is cascading Fern Creek Falls sprinting down the mountain to a rendez-vous with Reversed Creek. Fern Creek Falls is robust in early season but is much more impressive when looking up at it from various points near Silver Lake. At one mile and just shy of the falls, you'll come to a fork.

Bear right at the split to Fern Lake. Straight ahead leads to Yost Lake. Re-member the old saw, "Hiking is more about attitude that altitude." This is an excellent place to ponder that bit of trail wisdom as you struggle up an un-mercifully steep pitch for .25 mile. As you slog and pant past droopy-tipped hemlocks and fragrant junipers, take heart in knowing that the majority of the ascent is over when you reach a sweet little meadow. However, the hiking gods have one more short, punishing uphill to test your sense of humor before arriving at diminutive Fern Lake. This 800-foot-long gem at 9100 feet sits in a granite cup at the base of Carson Peak and San Joaquin Mountain. It's a lovely, photogenic locale to lollygag the day away or to rest before returning to the trailhead or moving on to Yost Lake.

Fern Lake is a good staging area for mountain climbers to bag the summit of Class 1 San Joaquin Mountain. From the 11,600-foot crest, splendid views of Mount Ritter, the Minarets and Banner Peak await those with experience and good physical conditioning. The route up San Joaquin's northwest slope is obvious at the head of the small cirque.

YOST LAKE

If you're visiting both lakes you'll need to walk 0.7 mile down to the junction and turn right (east). Yost Lake is 1.4 miles from the fork, involving a steady 940-foot climb. Crossing Fern Creek Falls might present a problem during snow melt—be careful. The east-trending ascent treats hikers to postcard perfect views of June Lakes Basin and surrounding territory. The lofty reddish peak looming above Silver Lake is Mount Wood. Views disappear as the trail threads a thickly forested ravine within earshot of Yost Creek. Bending south, your route follows the creek briefly before a gradual push to a junction. The left branch eventually reaches Glass Creek Meadow. If Yost Lake is your destination, bear right, pop over a low ridge and walk briefly down to petite Yost Lake, elevation 9100 feet. The lake, headwaters for Yost Creek, hunkers in a small basin below June Mountain.

Abundantly watered by rills and streams originating on June and San Joaquin Mountains, acres of marsh and flowery meadows grace the surrounding slopes. Yost Meadow just east of Yost Lake turnoff is the most lavish of all. Dark green grasses in midsummer host a sea of moisture-loving flowers. Although it's tempting to wade into their midst to be surrounded by such an extravagance of beauty, don't do it. High mountain flora are hardy but extremely vulnerable to damage by lug-soled boots. Please observe their beauty from a distance and don't pick them. Watch where you step and walk over or around little plants along the trail. Carry an Eastern Sierra wildflower book to identify the many varieties.

Return the way you came unless you're hiking to Glass Creek Meadow Trailhead. You might find the 2.4-mile trek back to the parking area even more scenic and enjoyable because you're not breathing so hard. Although the return trip is much less taxing on your cardiovascular system, the trail is just as steep as it was on the way up. Take your time and savor the wealth of scenery around you.

June Lakes Basin is more than just a gorgeous recreation paradise. Most visitors are unaware of its unusual geology. The Basin doesn't fit the characteristic pattern of glacier-scoured canyons. Rather than a vertical gouge from mountaintop to valley floor, this canyon curves like a horseshoe. A million years ago Rush Creek Glacier was the architect of this unique terrain. The 24-mile-square river of ice took a peculiar curved course, unlike the straightness of other glacier-cut canyons in the range. The loop's other singular aspect is the direction of Reversed Creek, aptly named because June Lake's outlet stream runs toward the mountains, flowing through the horseshoe-shaped canyon to Grant Lake and then on to Mono Lake.

ALTERNATE ROUTE TO FERN AND YOST LAKES

A trail across from the June Lake firehouse starts 300 feet higher than at Fern Creek. It angles up a moraine through the forest on the east slope of June Mountain for 2 miles. In early summer, blue-purple lupine blankets the hillside and perfumes the air with an exotic scent. The trail then runs along the moraine's nearly level crest. After you traverse June Mountain Ski Area, several meadows sport colorful flowers that change with the season.

Below Yost Lake the trail curves northward and soon reaches the fork to Yost Lake at 4.6 miles. You have options at this point: 1) return to June Lake 2) visit Fern Lake at 6.7 miles 3) and then hike out to the Fern Creek Trailhead for an 8.4-mile loop. Obviously, the loop can be taken in either direction. Don't forget to arrange a shuttle car.

GLASS CREEK MEADOW

Don't attempt this partially cross-country hike without a Mammoth Mountain topo or Tom Harrison's *Mammoth High Country Trail Map* or unless you are comfortable hiking off-trail. Note on the map that about one mile past Yost Lake junction the established trail at the head of a meadow swings to the left downhill to June Lake. You want to proceed straight ahead. The path is defined a bit after the June Lake turnoff. At the end of a long, lush meadow on your right, the path is faint to the saddle directly ahead of you. Beyond the saddle, locally called Yost Pass, from which you look down into Glass Creek watershed, there is no trail. Stay high and to the west (right) above the willow and aspen thickets in the draw leading to the drainage. When the willows thin out a little, drop down to the east toward and into the meadow with minimal bushwhacking. Skirt its north side and pick up the trail at the east end of the grassland down to the parking area by the creek (see Chapter 16).

Glass Creek Meadow
Ah, Wilderness!

◆ THE DETAILS

Getting There: Drive 3.7 miles south of the most southerly June Lakes junction. Turn right (west) on Glass Flow Road, Forest Road 2S10, and drive 2.7 miles to the unsigned trailhead. Where the road branches into three routes, do not cross the creek. Bear right and park above the creek near a wooden signboard.

Nearest Campground: Primitive camping at the trailhead—no facilities of any kind. Hartley Springs Campground, just off Glass Flow Road near Obsidian Dome, has primitive camping with tables, toilets, fire grills, no piped water.

Lodging/Services: June Lakes Loop has many choices. Try Boulder Lodge 760-648-7533 or Silver Lake Resort 760-648-7525 housekeeping cabins.

Further Info: Inyo National Forest, Mammoth Ranger Station 760-924-5500.

User Groups: Hikers only. Dogs OK on leash. No mountain bikes.

Hike Distance: 4 miles round trip to meadow, 6 miles round trip to end of meadow.

Difficulty: Moderate.

Best Time to Go: Early summer for flowers.

Cautions: Don't slog through the meadow when it's marshy in early season.

Elevation: 8170 feet at trailhead, 8800 feet at meadow.

Map: See page 120.

Other Maps: Tom Harrison's ***Mammoth High Country Trail Map***. **Ansel Adams Wilderness Map** incorrectly shows a trail linking Glass Creek Meadow and Yost Lake. It does not exist.

OF INTEREST

◆ A wonderful summer wildflower display in the Eastern Sierra's largest subalpine meadow.

◆ A fairly gentle hike compared to most Eastern Sierra trails.

◆ Newly designation wilderness at the headwaters of the Owens River.

◆ Nearby Obsidian Dome offers intriguing geology and great vistas from its top.

A day trip to huge, flower-packed Glass Creek Meadow does not involve a laborious hike up one of the eastside's formidable canyons. Although the primary focus of this book is to entice and guide people into these stupendous glacial troughs, I believe the meadow's environmental significance deserves to be broadcast. Visitors and locals need to experience the area and learn of its importance in the grand scheme of things. Situated between June Lake and Mammoth, the meadow is a lovely, unsullied ecological niche and a sanctuary for myriad life forms. I encourage you to invest a day in the Eastern Sierra's largest subalpine meadow.

Glass Creek Meadow, elevation 8800 feet, is a minute part of the newly designated 14,800-acre Owens River Headwaters addition to Ansel Adams Wilderness within Inyo National Forest. The addition also protects 15 miles along Deadman and Glass Creeks and Upper Owens River down to Owens River Ranch. Under the designations Wild and Scenic and Wilderness, the pristine source of the Eastern Sierra's most important stream would be safeguarded. Preservation of the Upper Owens is critical to a large population of wildlife and plants. For humans, an intact ecosystem is essential to the health of a tourist-based economy.

Situated just east of the Sierra Crest, Owens River Headwaters is a unique island of wet forest and meadow habitat in an arid sagebrush world. Because of its singular geographic location, the addition is a biologically rich and diverse region. Pacific moisture flowing over San Joaquin Ridge fosters a rare mixture of eastern and western Sierra flora. The ridge's relatively low elevation also provides a vital migration corridor for deer, endangered bighorn sheep and other animals. Furthermore, the Headwaters contains over 100 life-giving seeps and springs that sustain some of the most abundant riparian habitat in the Eastern Sierra.

Surrounded by forest and guarded by a regiment of snow-mantled peaks in the distance, Glass Creek Meadow is truly an enchanting landscape. After passing over a hot, glaring stretch of pumice-studded sand, the meadow is an unexpected, welcome oasis. A capillary-like network of streamlets nourishes the marshy environment. The expansive garden spot is home to dozens of seeps and springs, 40 species of butterflies, Yosemite toads, tree frogs and gazillions of wildflowers in July and August. Besides offering a peaceful refuge to man and beast, its size is surprising. Compared to a majority of smaller eastside meadows, Glass Creek Meadow seems about the size of Rhode Island!

Access to the trailhead is easy and short. Drive 3.7 miles south of the most southerly June Lake junction. Turn west (right) on Glass Flow Road, Forest Road 2S10, and pass Obsidian Dome at 1.5 miles. Take notice of this intriguing, 300-foot-high geological formation. Be sure to stop here after the hike and investigate the mile-long, knobby hill of volcanic glass. Take a short walk up the gated road to an abandoned pumice quarry topside. Explore the eerie, desolate moonscape and discover great views.

Continue 1.2 miles to where the road breaks into three routes. Do not cross the creek. Bear right and immediately reach a parking area and a few primitive, unofficial campsites just above the stream.

In 2004 there was no trailhead sign, but the route begins behind a post cautioning, "vehicular traffic is not allowed." Mellow at first, the path follows the right side of Glass Creek. Soon it steepens sharply as the trail penetrates a narrow ravine. Watch your footing lest you take a tumble into the stream. Sweet trailside flowers and the melody of cascading Glass Creek help you negotiate a quarter-mile of loose rock and sand.

The gradient abates considerably above the top of merry Glass Creek Falls and enters dry, sage-studded terrain. Follow the path, faint at times, on the uphill side of the creek. Over-the-shoulder views of Obsidian Dome are photo-worthy. Ascend gently through a glaring, barren, sandy land-

Glass Creek Falls

scape. Note the downed trees on your right with their roots pointing downhill instead of uphill. An avalanche on the opposite mountainside deposited them here much like driftwood on the beach after high tide. Top a little ridge around 1.5 miles and catch sight of the meadow, beckoning to you like an emerald green mirage at the end of a rather sterile landscape. Among the peaks in the distance, 11,600-foot-high San Joaquin Mountain rules the skyline.

Reach the big meadow at 2 miles and feast your eyes on the gorgeous and colorful, flowery scene. If you're a bit rusty, an Eastern Sierra wildflower guide will help you identify the many species thriving here. My guess is the mile-long meadow will lure you to walk across it. Be a responsible visitor and walk around it when the spongy grass is especially boggy in early season. In any case, never walk single file through the meadow if there is more than one of you. Spread out to prevent an unsightly web of trails and damage to the fragile, unspoiled setting.

Ah, wilderness . . . is it really so important? You bet it is, and more so every year. Within twenty years California's population is projected to burgeon to 50 million people. Think about what that means to wild places. Before heading back to civilization, give some thought to why you visit places such as Glass Creek Meadow. What drew you here? Why do you feel so calm and content when you wander in nature's wild embrace? What's here that nourishes your spirit? Protecting wild places is more than important. It's essential. Whether or not we recognize a yearning for wilderness, "We simply need that wild country be available to us, even if we never do more than drive to its edge and look in," said Wallace Stegner.

According to a recent statewide survey, 72 percent of California voters support permanent protection for more wilderness and wild rivers. Over the last two decades more than 700,000 acres—an area of unprotected wilderness about the size of Yosemite National Park—has been lost in California alone. Many more acres of public lands and miles of wild rivers remain at risk. Destructive threats include real estate development, logging, proliferation of illegal off-road vehicle use, ski resort development, road and dam construction, and mining.

Before leaving, take a long, last look around. Imagine this gorgeous, serene grassland scarred with off-road vehicle trails. Hear the snarl and whine of dirt bikes. Smell the exhaust fumes spewing from snowmobiles. Visualize rows of cabins and condos, power lines and paved roads. Wouldn't the meadow make a spectacular golf course? Just imagine the setting without wildflowers, without bird song, without the coyote's quavering howl, without pine-scented breezes, without concerts of toads and frogs. Given the destruction of other pristine locations in California, it's conceivable that it could have happened here or somewhere else within the 2009 wilderness addition. Remember the refrain from a 1970s Joni Mitchell song? "They paved paradise and put up a parking lot." If that seems far-fetched, perhaps paranoid, think about Tahoe, Mammoth and Yosemite Valley.

Tell your friends that wilderness is extremely important as homes for countless animals and plants that can't survive anywhere else, for clean air and drinking water, recreational opportunities, and economic benefits. California's rural regions once depended on resource extraction. Now, many people earn their living from tourism and recreation, which are dependent on healthy, intact ecosystems. Remember to keep in mind and to tell your friends that wilderness is for every one of us. It is not an exclusive, private playground for hikers and environmentalists. One person recently said to me, "We don't need anymore wilderness for those vegetarian hikers in Birkenstocks who live in Berkeley." Unfortunately, I suspect many people agree with that uninformed sentiment.

The core issues of wilderness protection are so much larger and more important than setting aside regions for the exclusive use of a relatively few people. It's about safeguarding California's biodiversity which provides ecological, recreational, aesthetic and economic benefits for all of us. It's about preserving unspoiled pieces of our rapidly vanishing, priceless natural heritage and its non-human inhabitants.

The Owens River Headwaters addition, part of Senator Barbara Boxer's Wild Heritage Act, was passed in 2009 and signed into law as part of the huge Omnibus Public Lands Management Act. With continued strong grassroots support, the addition permanently protects this wilderness, a reservation of peace for all creatures great and small, a haven of quiet past the end of the road.

If you're interested in joining Friends of the Inyo in preserving the wildlife, wild places, cultural and recreational values on public lands in the Eastern Sierra, call them at 760-873-6400, or visit their website, www.friendsoftheinyo.org.

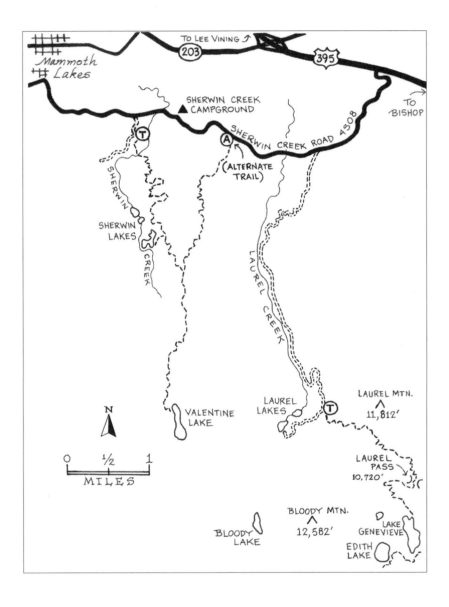

17

Laurel Canyon
A High Sierra Safari

◆ THE DETAILS

Getting There: Follow Highway 395 for one mile south from the Mammoth Lakes/Highway 203 intersection. Turn right (west) on Sherwin Creek Road and follow it 1.4 miles to Laurel Canyon Road (Road 4S86). From there, follow directions in the text.

Nearest Campground: Sherwin Creek Campground (see Chapter 19).

Lodging/Services: Call Mammoth Lakes Visitor Center 1-800-367-6572, or try Motel 6 760-934-6660 (1-800-4motel6).

Further Info: Inyo National Forest, Mammoth Ranger District and Visitor Center 760-924-5500.

User Groups: Hikers. Dogs OK on leash.

Hike Distance: Variable, but about 3 miles round trip to mining prospects on Bloody Mountain, 7 miles round trip to Lake Genevieve.

Difficulty: Moderately strenuous for Bloody Mountain, strenuous to Lake Genevieve.

Best Times to Go: Midsummer after snow melt through October. Fall colors are superb along Laurel Creek.

Cautions: Only high-clearance, four-wheel-drive vehicles driven by someone with off-road experience should attempt Laurel Canyon Road. Watch the weather! This is not a place to get caught in a storm.

Elevation: The drive, 7400 feet to 9770 feet; to Lake Genevieve, 9770 feet at trailhead to 10,720 feet to 10,000 feet and back; to Bloody Mountain, 9770 feet at trailhead to 11,200 feet.

Map: See page 128.

Other Maps: **Mammoth High Country Trail Map** by Tom Harrison is the best and most up to date.

OF INTEREST

◆ Dramatic four-wheel-drive road into a vast, little known canyon, another Mr. Toad's wild ride.

◆ Fascinating geology near the Long Valley Caldera.

◆ Grand vistas of the surrounding Eastern Sierra.

◆ Little known hikes to several alpine lakes.

Four miles southeast of Mammoth Lakes, an infrequently used route near Sherwin Creek Campground climbs a bone-jarring, crude, four-wheel-drive route to two alpine lakes in an astonishingly beautiful canyon. Although only a few miles as the raven flies from downtown Mammoth, Laurel Lakes seem light years away from civilization. The 5-mile-long road ascends a 1000-foot-high crescent-shaped moraine at the mouth of Laurel Canyon. Near road end a challenging trail leads to a full menu of matchless High Sierra scenery, interesting geology, knockout views and a litter of sun-spangled lakes.

The road, certainly a euphemism, was hacked out of the slope in 1955 to reach a tungsten mining claim at 11,200 feet on the north flank of Bloody Mountain. No longer used for its original purpose, the slender track is inarguably a dagger in the heart of wilderness. Its scar is obvious, and many of us environmentally oriented backcountry buffs lament destruction of the pristine wilderness the canyon once had. Nonetheless, like it or not, the road is there, and it does eliminate a 4.6-mile hike and a 2400-foot elevation gain.

I've come to accept the presence of these aging corridors that were built many decades ago. Although an outspoken advocate for no new roads in our forest and other wild places, I've made my peace with existing ones. Like Laurel Canyon, many of them aren't maintained and get rougher and less passable each year. And that's a good thing. One day Ma Nature will let loose with a rock slide to heal the wound on her mountainside, making the journey possible only to those willing and able to hike into this wildly scenic backcountry.

That said, if you don't have a high clearance four-wheel-drive vehicle, are a purist or a touch masochistic, don't drive. Instead, hump up the road to Laurel Lakes, elevation 9770 feet, and the trailhead to Lake Genevieve and other destinations in Inyo National Forest on the edge of John Muir Wilderness. Remember, however, to start at daybreak if you're hoofing it because it's a long, hot haul into the canyon.

This trail description assumes you are driving. If not, don't forget to tack on four-plus miles each way! One mile south of the Mammoth Lakes/Highway 395 junction, turn right (west) onto Sherwin Creek Road. Proceed 1.4 miles and turn left (south) on Road 4S86, Laurel Canyon Road. The majority of stock four-wheel-drive pickups and SUVs are capable of negotiating this route. In a few places, you will definitely need to use low range four-wheel drive both uphill and down. Because they lack a low range gear, all-wheel-drive vehicles should not attempt this road. It's an exciting and edgy (no pun intended) ride up the mountain and most assuredly adds another level of adventure to the outing.

Be prepared for a slow, bumpy ride while you climb the narrow shelf road, snake through a set of amazing zigzags and clink across a talus slope. If you only use your SUV in town or for freeway travel, do consider allowing someone with off road experience to take the wheel. Truthfully, the trip is not as scary as it may sound, especially if you are cautious, use good judgment and keep the pedal off the metal.

Beginning at 7400 feet and ending at nearly 10,000 feet, the road attacks an enormous, intact moraine left by Laurel Creek Glacier. Characteristic of Eastern Sierra gorges, the entrance is arid and populated by sagebrush and other flora at home in hot, water-robbed terrain. Novice travelers in the sunrise side of the range will be surprised by the lush landscape in the canyon's upper reaches. Not far from Sherwin Creek Road, streamside aspens, willows and pocket meadows come into view. Farther up the mountain, lodge pole and whitebark pines cling to the slopes. The rocky environment also hosts a colorful variety of wildflowers.

The majestic landscape of Laurel Canyon

Although you can drive the first mile or so without four-wheel drive, I recommend using it at the first switchback. The surface deteriorates and becomes rocky with poor traction. Just under a mile you'll pass a small brown building, a shack actually, containing equipment that monitors at great depth changes in Long Valley Caldera's magma chamber. The Mammoth region is seismically active and has an age-old history of volcanism and temblors. Swarms of earthquakes, carbon dioxide emissions and steam from fumaroles attest that Mammoth Mountain is still an active volcano. Scientists know without a doubt that the area is a work in progress, and the forces of nature are still fine-tuning the landscape. At the top of the switchbacks, enjoy splendid vistas of Mammoth Lakes and the Sierra skyline as you enter Laurel Canyon.

Rattle across a cattle guard at 1.7 miles and begin paralleling Laurel Creek.

Bear right around a deeply rutted section of the road. At 2.2 miles a short spur drops into a small meadow at 8400 feet. Here, serenaded by the creek where aspen leaves flutter like green butterflies, is a charming, primitive camping area. It's also a picturesque location to take a break and snap a few photos. If the road is not to your liking, this can be a turnaround point. Or, park and walk the remaining 2.4 miles to the Lake Genevieve Trailhead or 2.8 miles to Laurel Lakes. Please don't litter. Remember, there's no one to pack out your trash but you.

Beyond the idyllic riparian setting, ignore a side road leading down into the meadow. Soon, the rocky mining access road gets seriously steep and briefly travels over a stretch of loose talus. At this spot, I couldn't help but wonder if this might be the moment Mother Nature would decide to do a little landscape rearranging! In early summer expect to see quite an extensive array of wildflowers—lupine, Indian paintbrush, scarlet penstemon and pennyroyal among them. The rather exotic white blossoms of prickly poppies and the bright yellow flower clusters of rabbit brush are a treat later in summer and early fall.

About 3.7 miles in, a switchback orients you northward, and without warning a spectacular vista jumps out at you. Stop here to enjoy it. Far below is the sprawling town of Mammoth Lakes and the ghostly Mono Craters. Note the peaks of the Sierra Crest above Yosemite Park's eastern border. Pause to ponder the Long Valley Caldera, part of which you can see from here. The caldera is a 20-mile-long elliptical basin, or depression, created by the collapse of the immense Long Valley volcano.

A titanic eruption occurred 760,000 years ago, spewing 150 cubic miles of fiery lava and ash over the landscape. Black clouds of superheated ash rose eight miles into the atmosphere and most likely darkened the sky for a very long time. Smaller ash particles caught in the jet stream traveled as far east as Kansas and Nebraska.

A 500-foot-thick blanket of rhyolite ash completely buried 350 square miles, overriding hills and filling canyons. In comparison, the eruption of Mount St. Helens amounted to no more than a burp. The ancient and still active caldera is bounded by Laurel and McGee Mountains to the south, Glass and Bald Mountains to the north, San Joaquin Mountain to the west and Long Valley to the east.

Continuing on, Laurel Mountain, elevation 11,872 feet, looms above the road, and the 12,552-foot presence of Bloody Mountain presides over the canyon headwall. A relatively wide place at 4.6 miles indicates the start of a steep and scenic 3.5-mile trail to Lake Genevieve. The path, eventually terminating at Convict Lake, traverses a lake-filled paradise with utterly heart-stopping views.

Either turn around and park at the trailhead indicated by a wooden post, or if the road beyond isn't obstructed by rocks or snow, drive a short distance to a flat, wide section. Here, at 10,050 feet, you'll find more room to turn around. This spot gives new meaning to a "scenic turnout." The vista from this little spur offers a mini-course in High Sierra geology. Ahead, Laurel Creek Glacier was born in the womb-like cirque more than 25,000 years ago. The contrast between the bowl's pale gray granite and the brick-red metamorphic rocks of an unnamed peak is stunning.

To the northeast, the deeply corrugated, multihued face of Laurel Mountain holds the eye. Neither its shape nor color seems real, as if both a sculptor and a painter created its form and coloring. An important moment in western climbing history occurred on Laurel Mountain with the first belayed rope climb in the Sierra Nevada during the peak's first ascent in 1930. The soft green waters of Lower and Upper Laurel Lakes lay 230 feet below. The air smells wild and fresh, and Sierra sunshine warms you here like nowhere else. Even the most jaded hiker will be smitten by the lavish scenery.

Even if the way is clear, I strongly suggest parking and walking down to Upper Laurel. The hairpin twists beyond the "scenic turnout" are very rough and very steep. The first switchback is tight, necessitating very careful maneuvering. Why bother driving when it's only 0.5-mile from Genevieve Trailhead to the lake? Besides, you'll surely be ready to get out and walk.

On the walk down, take notice of a trail, actually a continuation of the road, that starts up Bloody Mountain. Look up and you'll see the route slicing back and forth across the slope's northeast flank. The sole object of this old track you just drove and the one you see leading skyward was to reach the Hard Point Prospect. After an exploration of sparkling Laurel Lakes, take a hike up Bloody Mountain to get a feel for what tungsten miners had to deal with. One can only hope they appreciated the austere and majestic scenery characteristic of the environment at tree line.

After trying to coax a few trout out of the lakes or taking a lunch break, get your boots on the hard scrabble road. Bloody Mountain was not named for its dark red color. Its name derived from a fierce gun battle in 1871 between a posse and escaped convicts that occurred in the general vicinity. If you're unaccustomed to high elevation, you'll notice that the air at timberline always seems to lose weight. Take it easy and find a comfortable pace. Many years and many miles ago, my Sierra mentor advised, "If you're in a hurry to get from here to there, you'll miss where you are."

The mountain's severe landscape has a savage beauty that appeals to devout High Sierraphiles. And, if you have a penchant for silence, this is the place to indulge in solitude. Starting at 10,000 feet, hike up as far as you'd like or until the route ends at the mining claims 1200 feet above. Today it's hard for most of us to fathom the quest for tungsten, a mineral many people are unfamiliar with. During World War II and the Korean War years, however, it was in great demand to alloy with steel. The extremely high melting point made it an invaluable component in the manufacture of weaponry and armor-proof products.

Prospectors found exposed tungsten (scheelite) deposits on the near vertical face of Bloody Mountain and built a road to their claims in 1955. It's a gross understatement to say mining was not easy at this location. The ore bodies could only be reached by means of ropes and ladders tethered into solid rock. Due to the obvious and extraordinary access problems and mediocre quantity and quality of the deposits, not an ounce of tungsten was ever mined on Bloody Mountain. The improbable road to the prospects has been impassable to vehicles for years, but it affords hikers a rare opportunity to experience a unique and dramatically scenic Sierra destination.

A few campsites sit among the rocks and pines just above upper Laurel Lake. Although there are fire rings, campfires are not legal at this elevation. To avoid brisk winds and cold nights, consider camping lower down among the aspens along Laurel Creek. Climbers will be tempted to have a go at Bloody Mountain, as did the legendary Norman Clyde in 1928. The northeast ridge, south and southwest slopes are all Class 2.

Return to your parked vehicle and SLOWLY wind down the mountain.

Upper Laurel Lake near the end of Laurel Creek Road

Personally, I'm thankful the road feels like I'm riding in a blender on the "chop" setting. Otherwise this magnificent canyon would be overrun with visitors.

Said early Sierra Club leader Elmo Robinson in 1930, "The value of the Sierra lies in its being what it is . . . a region of marvelous scenic beauty, moderately difficult of access. Let us remember that there will always be those who know that the most marvelous views are seen only after physical effort to obtain them, who prefer intimacy with the mountains to their own personal comfort . . . Let us save a place for them."

18
Lake Genevieve
Climb to a Crest-Kissing Gem

◆ THE DETAILS

Getting There: One mile south of Mammoth Lakes/Highway 395 junction, turn right (west) onto Sherwin Creek Road. Proceed 1.4 miles and turn left (south) on Road 4S86, Laurel Canyon Road. Drive 4.6 miles to the trailhead, indicated by a wooden post. See Chapter 17 for important information about negotiating this road.

Nearest Campground: Sherwin Creek Campground (fee) has 87 forested sites near the creek with water, tables, flush toilets, fire rings and barbecues. Some sites can be reserved through www.recreation.gov. Open May to October. Dogs on leash OK. Close to trailhead and Mammoth.

Lodging/Services: Call Mammoth Lakes Visitor Center 1-800-367-6572, or try Motel 6 760-934-6660 (1-800-4motel6).

Further Info: Inyo National Forest, Mammoth Ranger District and Visitor Center 760-924-5500.

User Groups: Hikers only. Dogs OK on leash.

Hike Distance: 7 miles round trip from trailhead in Laurel Canyon. 15 miles round trip from Convict Lake (see Chapter 20).

Difficulty: Strenuous.

Best Times to Go: Midsummer for wildflowers, through October for flaming fall color.

Cautions: Four-wheel-drive and high-clearance vehicles only. If you can see patches of snow on the road up-canyon or a storm approaching, don't go! There are only a couple of marginal turnouts. See Chapter 17 for full description.

Elevation: 9770 feet at trailhead in Laurel Canyon. Ascends to 10,720 feet at summit, then descends to 10,000 feet at Lake Genevieve.

Map: See page 128.

Other Map: **Mammoth High Country Trail Map** by Tom Harrison is best.

OF INTEREST

◆ Spectacular views are the pay-off for a steep climb.

◆ Secluded, little-visited High Country lakes.

◆ A sublime shuttle hike is possible, offering one of the Eastern Sierra's most scenic and memorable outings.

Lake Genevieve and the dramatic peaks around it

If you need a big dose of High Country to revitalize your spirit and get your head and body in the same zip code, a hike or backpack to large and lovely Lake Genevieve in John Muir Wilderness could be the remedy to cure what ails you. There are two ways to reach this secluded, half-mile-long beauty at the foot of Bloody Mountain southeast of Mammoth. Both are demanding, high elevation journeys requiring considerable climbing. However, the scenic rewards for all the puffing and panting compensate for the sweat equity invested in either trail. As veteran back country ramblers say, "Hiking is more about attitude than altitude."

The shorter and less difficult way to Lake Genevieve starts at a trailhead 4.6 miles up Laurel Canyon Road, a very rough track clinging to the mountainside. Read Chapter 17 for details. A longer route with a hefty elevation gain threads Convict Canyon above Convict Lake (see Chapter 20). It's a demanding 15-mile round trip, suitable as a day hike for only the most energetic hiker in top physical condition. Other options besides out and back hikes from either trailhead are possible, but this guide speaks to the 7-mile round trip between Laurel Canyon and Lake Genevieve.

The unmaintained access to Lake Genevieve Trailhead in Laurel Canyon is not for everyone. Some will find the primitive road intimidating. It's narrow, rocky and extremely choppy, certainly beyond the capability of an ordinary passenger car. Please don't attempt this route without a four-wheel-drive, high-clearance vehicle. Nevertheless, the drive to the trailhead is chock-full of wondrous Eastern Sierra scenery. Personally, this sojourn feeds my adventurous spirit and deepens the experience of hiking to Lake Genevieve. If you're willing to work for your scenery, wilderness will open its heart to you.

A wood post marks the trailhead, where the rudimentary road is just wide enough to carefully turn around. Hug the mountain when you park, leaving the roadway clear. Before tackling the steep slope, take time to survey the neighborhood. In case you haven't noticed, this is a perfect example of off the beaten path, definitely the road less traveled that you read about in outdoor publications. You're not just looking at a dramatic mountain scene; you are actually in it, a part of it. Walk briefly up the road to a flat spur and behold the Sierra's spectacular geology and halcyon setting of Laurel Lakes near the headwall. The Jovian scale of the landscape is profoundly moving.

Heading generally eastward, the trail to Lake Genevieve immediately takes you uphill on a series of switchbacks. Around 0.75 mile the path relaxes its upward course in favor a gentler grade as you enjoy marvelous, open views. Start another switchbacking ascent to a shallow saddle between Bloody and Laurel Mountains and pass through a peculiar bowl formation. The pool at the bottom—questionable potability—is created by snowmelt. Beautiful wildflowers live here surrounded by colorful, tilted bands of rock.

At 2.2 miles the trail starts an easterly climb out of the strange basin, again regaling you with expansive vistas. Stunted whitebark pines, more like shrubs, hang on for dear life on the windy, exposed ridges. A half-mile farther, gain the top of a 10,720-foot ridge, unofficially called Laurel Pass. Park on a rock and soak up the Sierra's immensity and diversity. Find yourself in a vast, dramatic landscape as unspoiled and lovely as the Sierra affords. The view to the north takes in the extensive Long Valley Caldera—a depression caused by the collapse of a gargantuan volcano—while the view east includes Crowley Lake and the White Mountains. The most riveting sight is an incredible shot of Convict Lake 3000 feet below.

Surrounded by the deep carnelian slopes of Laurel and Bloody Mountains, big and beautiful Lake Genevieve to the south is a living picture postcard. On the day I first saw the 42-acre lake from above, its color left me dumbstruck. Dark as obsidian where cloud-shadowed and malachite in full sun, I couldn't stop staring at it. The unusual, two-toned kaleidoscope changed constantly as fat, puffy cumulus formations scudded by. Colorful, fantastic convoluted rock layering in the mountains added to the visual drama. These are the kinds of serendipitous moments that leave hikers with the post-wilderness blues after coming down from the High Country.

Before tearing yourself away from this eagle's-eye view of the world, look right at a small no-name lake north of Edith Lake, quite easily reached by following Genevieve's inlet stream. Great campsites can be found at Edith Lake and nearby Cloverleaf Lake. Both are just a short jaunt from Lake Genevieve. Take stock of your energy and decide whether this ridgetop perch will be your turn around spot or if you want to switchback about one mile and 800 feet down to Lake Genevieve. If you do, remember it's a mile and 800 feet uphill on the way back.

For those choosing to press on, zigzag downhill toward Genevieve. Backpackers will find good campsites in the grass just above the lake. Campfires are not permitted at this elevation. Pitch your tent at least 40 paces away from the water. Day hikers, after a rest, will reverse the hike to the trailhead in Laurel Canyon.

For a superb grand tour of Laurel and Convict Canyons, strong hikers should give serious thought to continuing down the mountain to Convict Lake's incredibly beautiful setting at 7600 feet, about 7.5 miles distant from the south end of Lake Genevieve. With a little planning and a car shuttle, sturdy hikers will undoubtedly find this sublime, but long, two-canyon trek one of the most scenic and memorable outings in the Eastern Sierra. The trip can be done in reverse if a formidable uphill hike is to your liking and within your physical ability. Only an absolute iron man/woman should think about a round trip between the two canyons. The map will reveal other possibilities and destinations between the two canyons for both knapsackers and backpackers.

19
Sherwin Canyon
From Sagebrush to Subalpine Splendor

◆ THE DETAILS

Getting There: Drive Highway 395 south from Mammoth Lakes junction (Highway 203) for 1.5 miles, then turn right (west) onto signed Sherwin Creek Road. Pass Sherwin Creek Campground and continue 4 miles to a signed spur road for Sherwin Lakes Trailhead. Turn left and continue 0.3 mile to a fork. Bear left for 0.1 mile to the trailhead, which has toilets but no water.

Nearest Campground: Sherwin Creek Campground (fee) has 87 forested sites near the creek with water, tables, flush toilets, fire rings and barbecues. Some sites can be reserved through www.recreation.gov. Open May to October. Dogs on leash OK. Close to trailhead and Mammoth.

Lodging/Services: Mammoth Lakes has a plethora of amenities. Call Mammoth Lakes Visitor Bureau at 1-800-367-6572.

Further Info and Permits: Inyo National Forest, Mammoth Ranger District and Visitor Center 760-924-5500.

User Groups: Hikers, equestrians. Dogs OK on leash. No mountain bikes beyond wilderness boundary.

Hike Distance: 4.6 miles round trip to Sherwin Lakes, 9.6 miles round trip to Valentine Lake.

Difficulty: Moderate to Sherwin Lakes, strenuous to Valentine Lake.

Best Times to Go: May to October.

Cautions: Permits required for overnight stays. Practice zero impact techniques.

Elevation: 7840 feet at trailhead. 8600 feet at Sherwin Lakes, 9710 feet at Valentine Lake.

Map: See page 128.

Other Maps: USGS 7.5-minute Bloody Mountain topo, or *John Muir Wilderness Map.*

Winter Sports: Mammoth Mountain above Mammoth Lakes boasts a huge annual snow pack (48 feet in 2005!) and awesome terrain with a 3000-foot vertical drop from top to bottom. Snow hounds of all abilities and styles can play from November to June at Mammoth.

OF INTEREST

◆ Close to Mammoth Lakes, but hike leads to lightly visited lakes.

◆ Eight lakes tucked into one canyon.

◆ Panoramic vistas of the Mammoth Crest and Mammoth Lakes area.

Mammoth Lakes, six hours north of Los Angeles and three hours south of Reno, is an extraordinarily scenic portion of the 400-mile-long Sierra Nevada range. The bustling resort town of Mammoth Lakes sits roughly in the center of an area known as Mammoth Lakes Sierra, which stretches between Rock Creek Canyon and Lundy Canyon. The town sprawls below Mammoth Mountain and a picturesque, lake-filled basin. The territory surrounding Mammoth offers some of the finest hiking and winter sports in the Sierra and lures millions of visitors annually.

In the late nineteenth century, however, the magnet was gold and silver. A brief bonanza in 1877 and 1878 attracted thousands of Argonauts to the beautiful mountains. Activity centered around a mining camp called Mammoth City, named for Mammoth Mine on Red Mountain, but after the boom fizzled, it was changed to Mammoth Lakes. Generally, the town and area are known simply as Mammoth. By 1881, only a few diehard miners and ghost settlements remained. On the heels of departed miners came ranchers from sun-baked Owens Valley who grazed sheep and cattle in the lush meadows during summer.

An entirely different breed of pioneers discovered Mammoth's real treasures in the early 1900s. Instead of gold, the early settlers focused on the riches that were so abundantly present in this pristine mountain landscape. Fishing, hiking, camping, hunting, mountaineering, photography and horseback riding drew summer visitors to Mammoth. Right behind them flocked businessmen to service their needs. The completion of a modern highway in 1937 allowed even greater visitation to Mammoth's sublime scenery and plentiful recreational opportunities.

However it was lots of snow that lingered for half the year that really ignited the tourist boom. Ever since an avid young skier named Dave McCoy built and operated Mammoth's first permanent rope ski tow, the town has never stopped growing. You can find every visitor service imaginable at this year-round town. Mammoth Lakes, full-time population of 7000, is a busy urban community covering what once was a huge meadow. The 3500-acre ski and snowboarding area on Mammoth Mountain draws 1.6 million visitors each year. Summer and fall attract almost as many tourists when 1.2 people come to enjoy fair weather pursuits.

Although Mammoth teems with people, it is possible to get away from it all. There are many easy to challenging hiking destinations from Lakes Basin into the backcountry. The farther you move away from these thirteen lovely lakes, the more seclusion you'll find. Good guidebooks specific to the region detail the hikes and activities available in the entire region.

Trees grow on an island in Upper Sherwin Lake.

This chapter details an excellent canyon hike not far from the city, a 4.8-mile trek through Sherwin Canyon to Valentine Lake. In spite of a trailhead virtually within Mammoth's city limits, Valentine Lake at the southeastern foot of Mammoth Crest in John Muir Wilderness is lightly visited. In case you're wondering, its name has nothing to do with Cupid or February 14. It was named for Los Angeles businessman W.L. Valentine, one of the original owners of exclusive Valentine Camp built in Old Mammoth in 1920. Nonetheless, it is a sweetheart of a lake in a dramatic, glacier-carved setting. Less than 3 miles in, the Sherwin Lakes provide a scenic stopping point if the hike to Valentine seems beyond your endurance level.

There are two ways to access Sherwin Canyon Trailhead. Old Mammoth Road on the edge of town will get you there. Or, an alternative to driving into Mammoth is to turn west off Highway 395 onto Sherwin Creek Road (4S08), 1.5 miles south of the Highway 203 intersection. The landmark east of the highway is Hot Creek Fish Hatchery. Follow gravel Sherwin Creek Road 4 miles past the campground to the signed Sherwin Lakes spur. (1.3 miles past the spur, Sherwin Creek Road intersects Old Mammoth Road.) You'll find trailhead parking next to a restroom, but no water.

Under a thin canopy of Jeffrey pine and white fir, sagebrush and its frequent companion, yellow-blossomed mule ears, line the path that soon dips to cross Sherwin Creek on a footbridge. Pass a trail on the left that leads to a private camp and begin gradually working your way up an 800-foot-high moraine. A series of long, sweeping zigzags through the forest takes you to the crest at 1.8 miles. Good photo ops of Mammoth Lakes, volcanic domes south of Mono Lake and the distant White Mountains appear as you ascend the moraine that blocks the mouth of Sherwin Canyon.

After you top out at 8640 feet, enjoy a stretch of downhill and level walking plus a grand view of hulking Mammoth Mountain, elevation 11,053 feet, to the west. Well below the trail the three smallest of the five Sherwin Lakes nestle behind the moraine you just surmounted. If you want to visit them, wait until you reach the upper lakes and follow the outlet stream down to them. The lakes are little, pretty and secluded. They and many other natural features in the vicinity were named for L. C. Sherwin, pioneer settler in Round Valley in the 1860s.

The trail bends around a knob around 2.25 miles and shortly reaches the first of the two largest Sherwin Lakes. It's a very pleasant spot for a break or a little toe wiggling in the chilly water. In early season water may nudge the trail, and depending on the depth of the snow pack, the two lakes may flood their short connecting stream and become one. Moving on, proceed through the trees and boulders and watch for a junction in .25 mile. An easy-to-miss wooden sign tacked to a tree directs you left (southeast) for Valentine Lake and right (west) to a short spur to the uppermost Sherwin Lake, 800 feet long.

The trail to Valentine Lake undulates through sparse forest cover and immense Sierra junipers before crossing an aspen-lined creeklet. Climbing again, the trail intersects the old Valentine Lake trail coming up on the left from a secondary trailhead along Sherwin Creek Road. Although shorter, the old track is much steeper, less scenic, and very dusty. It also passes by a YMCA camp. Remember to bear left here on the return trip or you will find yourself far from your vehicle. The path briefly levels before climbing again as you enter John Muir Wilderness at 3.1 miles. The trail offers little respite in the remaining distance to Valentine Lake cradled beneath the canyon headwall.

Upper Sherwin Lake

The creekside trail rises moderately into a little valley and through a marshy area starred with a host of flowers, including the elegant Sierra rein orchid.

Another stint of climbing greets you after the wildflower garden. Cross a tributary creek and catch sight of Lost Lake below the trail to the west (right), another secluded gem in Sherwin Canyon accessible by a short cross-country jaunt. Splendid east-facing peaks on the crest accompany you on the way into the narrowing canyon.

Around 4 miles walk past a grass and red heather-rimmed pond and brace yourself for a tough set of twenty switchbacks near a waterfall below Valentine Lake's outlet. As you trudge steeply uphill on this final pitch, Sherwin Creek takes a header through the boulder-choked defile. The reward for 4.8 miles of heavy breathing is Valentine Lake, a rock-bound beauty at 9710 feet. Truly a stunner, Valentine sits in a granite basin at the very end of Sherwin Canyon.

No alpine puddle, the elliptical lake is deep and 2300 feet long, surrounded on three sides by the soaring, perpendicular cliffs of Mammoth Crest. The crest flags the boundary between Fresno and Mono Counties and Inyo and Sierra National Forests. Cross the outlet and settle in for a long lunch break. The serene setting is guaranteed to capture your attention for hours. Because of the terrain, campsites are limited, and backpackers need to find one at least 100 feet (40 paces) from the water. If you must have a fire, keep it small in existing rings. Camp stoves are preferable.

Before leaving, scramble up a low knoll near the outlet for panoramic north-south vistas. Another option is to maneuver over slabs of rock and investigate Valentine's south end where twin inlet streams from Mammoth Crest enter the lake. Anglers will find this spot a happy hunting ground for brook trout.

20

Convict Canyon
Sparkling Waters, Towering Peaks

◆ THE DETAILS

Getting There: From Highway 395 4.4 miles south of Mammoth Lakes exit, turn west on Convict Lake Road and drive 2.5 miles. As you near the lake, the road splits. The easy hike starts at the end of the left fork on the south side of the lake, while the strenuous hike leaves from the hikers' parking lot on the right fork. Day hikers can start up Convict Canyon from the end of Convict Lake Road, but overnight parking is prohibited.

Nearest Campground: Convict Lake Campground has 88 sites with piped water, open late April through October. Dogs OK on leash. No reservations.

Lodging/Services: Convict Lake Resort has housekeeping cabins set in a stand of aspens not far from the lake. The restaurant serves excellent food, and there is a small well-stocked store. Showers are available for a fee. Convict Lake Resort 800-992-2260. Write them at Route 1, Box 204, Mammoth Lakes, CA 93546.

Further Info: Inyo National Forest, Mammoth Ranger District 760-924-5500.

User Groups: Hikers and horses. Dogs OK on leash.

Hike Distance: 2-mile loop around Convict Lake. Convict Lake Trail: 6 miles round trip to ford, 10 miles round trip to Mildred Lake, 12 miles round trip to Lake Dorothy, 15 miles round trip to Lake Genevieve.

Difficulty: Easy for lake loop, strenuous to very strenuous for all other destinations.

Cautions: Do not attempt to ford Convict Creek at 3 miles unless its flow is low.

Best Times to Go: Midsummer for wildflowers, September to early October for autumn color.

Elevation: 7600 feet at trailhead. 2675 feet elevation gain to Lake Dorothy.

Other Maps: Best is **Mammoth High Country Trail Map** by Tom Harrison, or USGS 7.5-minute Convict Lake and Bloody Mountain topos.

OF INTEREST

◆ Immense Convict Lake offers a dramatic setting.

◆ Choice of short, easy hikes or a rugged climb to numerous alpine lakes.

◆ Excellent food and lodging at Convict Lake Resort.

Large, sparkling Convict Lake nestles at the foot of sheer metamorphic cliffs rising to jagged peaks. Don't let the drab, sagebrush-dotted entrance to this deep glacial canyon mislead you. Enter it and discover exposed layers of brightly colored, tilted and folded rock formations ranging from light gray to rich, reddish brown. Hikers, campers and anglers come to this majestic environment to immerse themselves in the relative solitude of a backcountry trail leading to several alpine lakes in John Muir Wilderness.

Called *Witsonapah* by Paiutes and *Monte Diablo Lake* by early settlers, the lake's tranquil high desert setting offers no clues to its violent moment in history 134 years ago or to how its landmarks were named. The lake, canyon and creek were renamed after one of the West's most dramatic jailbreaks and gun battles ended here.

On September 17, 1871, twenty-nine murderers, horse thieves, and train robbers effectively staged a bloody and deadly prison break from the state penitentiary in Carson City, Nevada. Armed with weapons stolen from prison stores, the inmates split up. Heading south, six of them set off for Arizona where with other renegades they "expected to live among the Indians and rob trains." En route they stole horses and brutally murdered and disfigured a teen-aged mail rider from Aurora, Nevada, whom they mistakenly identified as a prison guard who had shot two fellow inmates.

Posses from Aurora and Benton quickly assembled and rode off in hot pursuit. Robert Morrison, a merchant and posse member, first spotted the fugitives at Monte Diablo Creek, now Convict Creek, five days after their escape. In true Wild West fashion, a ferocious gunfight erupted in Convict Canyon between the cornered desperadoes and posse members. Using superior high-powered prison rifles, the outlaws wounded one of the posse, shot four horses out from under them, and killed their Indian guide.

As Morrison dismounted to take cover from wildly flying bullets, he was hit in the side. Outgunned, the posse left him and retreated from the immediate vicinity. When the wounded Morrison attempted to shoot Moses Black, perhaps the most vicious of the six, his pistol misfired, revealing his position in the bushes along the creek. With Morrison exposed and too feeble to try another shot, Black killed him with a bullet through the head. Later that day his body was taken to Benton where he was given a Masonic funeral. Ironically, Morrison was buried in a new suit he had just bought for his wedding. Lofty Mount Morrison, elevation 12,286 feet, was named in memory of this brave, slain merchant from nearby Benton.

Of the six fugitives, Burke and Cockerill were caught in southern Nevada. The wounded 18-year-old Roberts was arrested at Pine Creek where Black and Morton had abandoned him. Ten days after the breakout, Morton and Black were taken into custody by a Bishop posse in the sand hills near Round Valley. Charlie Jones, convicted murderer, was never caught.

Guarded by Bishop citizens, Roberts, Black and Morton were loaded in a wagon headed back to Carson City when outside of town some armed, masked riders commandeered the wagon. Stopping at a cabin in a nearby meadow, the makeshift jury questioned each man for two hours before voting on his fate. The vigilantes decreed that Black and Morton should be hanged. Spared the rope by a split vote, young Roberts was returned to prison.

After the so-called trial, the vigilantes hung ropes from a beam at one end of the cabin and placed nooses around the convicts' necks. The wagon served as a portable scaffold, and as it moved forward, the lives of these two danger-ous scofflaws ended. In the final analysis, eighteen of the twenty-nine escaped inmates were either killed or returned to jail within two months of the break-out. Well over a century has passed since the wild frontier incident occurred, and except for the name, there is nothing to remind us of that violent encoun-ter in Convict Canyon.

Convict Lake and towering peaks

THE HIKES

Convict Lake attains its ultimate grandeur when its abundant quaking aspens, the West's most flamboyant fall foliage trees, put on their show, but it offers gorgeous hikes all summer as well. Leaf peepers pilgrimage to this mountain shrine in autumn to behold sprawling groves of aspen flow-ing down the slopes in avalanches of brassy hues and to savor flaming is-lands of gold, orange and crimson on canyon floors and along stream banks. The dazzling color display is all the more magical because it is fleeting and unpredictable. Generally, the intensity of fall color in High Country happens between late September and early October, but one heavy windstorm can quickly defoliate a grove.

Two hikes that explore this canyon range from very easy to quite strenuous. By no means do you have to be a long-distance backcountry hiker to witness the magnificent mountain landscape, and the fall foliage show if your timing is right, around the lake. For less conditioned walkers, take the easy, mile-long path that begins at the road end on the left (south) shore of the lake. Follow it around the south shoreline to the inlet stream at the head of the lake. On the way, watch for the rare copper birch, named for the unusual color of its bark. Where Convict Creek tumbles into the lake, you'll find a great picnic spot at a gravelly beach. Cross the inlet's many rivulets on a boardwalk and head north to meet the Convict Lake Trail along the lake's north shore. To the left, the trail ascends steeply toward the backcountry of John Muir Wilderness. To complete the easy walk, turn right and loop around the lake's northwestern shore for one mile for another perspective of this colorful canyon, or return the way you came.

A much more strenuous trail starts near the resort and flanks the lake's northwestern shoreline into the canyon bisecting its headwall. As you enter the gorge on a steady ascent along Convict Creek, set an easy, comfortable pace that allows you to appreciate the bountiful wildflowers of summer or the brilliant autumn colors. After fording a tributary, you enter John Muir Wilderness. Towering peaks surround you as the trail skirts the base of Laurel Mountain, elevation 11,812 feet. To the west the rich reddish-brown slopes of Bloody Mountain dominate the skyline. The fanged Sierra Crest flanks it on the left, culminating at massive and rounded Red Slate Mountain, 13,163 feet elevation, the highest peak for miles. The rim of this glacial trough you're ascending is topped by Mount Morrison to the east and Mount Baldwin up canyon.

Be aware that 3 miles from the trailhead a tributary cascades down from Lake Genevieve and merges with Convict Creek to create a VERY DANGER-OUS ford. Several attempts to span the creek have failed. The Forest Service has given up trying to keep a bridge in place because the bridge has always washed out due to the combined, hard-charging force of the two streams. Before you undertake this hike, especially during peak snowmelt, inquire at the resort's store if it's passable. If not, let good judgment rule and DO NOT attempt to cross the icy, swift stream. Instead, postpone your trip. In late summer or autumn, you'll likely have no trouble crossing, although you may get a little wet.

If you can safely ford, another 2 miles of hiking brings you to Mildred Lake below Mount Baldwin. While chugging up the steep, scenery-rich trail, see if you can find some fossilized sea lilies (crinoids). Theses critters once lived in the shallow ocean that covered the area. Along the path and in the creek just below the lake, look sharp for black rocks imprinted with tiny, round, grayish formations. What you're holding in your hand lived here about 300 million years ago.

Long and beautiful Mildred Lake rests at the bottom end of a U-shaped glacial canyon. Since the glacier melted thousands of years ago, the valley has been slowly filling up with stream-borne sediments, creating lush meadows and marshes. Sometime in the distant future Mildred Lake will be known as Mildred Meadow. Such is the natural progression of change in the environment. Experi-

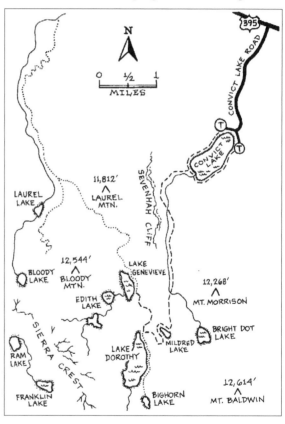

enced cross-country ramblers will want to explore Bright Dot Lake over the hill to the east of Mildred.

The trail circles around Mildred and climbs 500 feet to the lower end of Lake Dorothy, a huge, 250-foot-deep lake wondrously backdropped by Mammoth Crest. If this is your destination, find a spot to rest and soak up the scenery before returning. Camping is not permitted at this lake. If you're moving on, a left turn at the junction traces the lake's eastern shore. Continue 1.5 miles to Dorothy's far end where a stiff, 400-foot, 0.25-mile climb puts you at Bighorn Lake, elevation 10,630 feet. At Bighorn begin a short cross-country trek to remote Wit-So-Nah-Pah Lake and Constance Lake. In a stunning setting, Constance nestles against the base of spectacular Red Slate Mountain.

A right hand turn at the junction at the lower end of Dorothy crosses the outlet stream, pops over a low pass and descends to Lake Genevieve (see Chapter 18) in about 1.5 miles. Pause atop the pass and slowly scan this outrageously beautiful, colorful alpine mountainscape. Looking back (south) toward Mildred, the architecture of the glacial canyon above is as obvious as it is dramatic. Walking on, reach the southern tip of Lake Genevieve and climb to oval-shaped Edith Lake and Cloverleaf Lake, 0.6 and one mile respectively. In 2004 camping was not allowed at Genevieve. Check with the Forest Service for other overnight sites or if regulations at Genevieve and Dorothy have been modified.

There is so much to see in this magnificent section of the Eastern Sierra that it's a tough decision where to stop and turn around. Whatever your choice, be sure to allow ample time to complete the journey before dark. To do it justice, Convict Canyon should be hiked yearly, alternating between summer and fall. A backpack trip, of course, allows you to spend quality time in the area. A base camp at Mildred Lake is an ideal place from which to take day trips to the many lakes in the neighborhood. While your trip is in the planning stage, study the map for a few travel options besides an out and back excursion. Be sure to ask the Forest Service where it's legal to camp.

McGee Creek Canyon
Scenic Splendor beneath Rugged Ramparts

◆ THE DETAILS

Getting There: Turn west off Highway 395 8.5 miles south of the Mammoth Lakes/Highway 203 junction, 6.4 miles north of Tom's Place. Drive McGee Creek Road for 3.9 miles, passing a campground and pack station, to road's end and trailhead parking, where there are toilets, but no water. The trail begins behind the information board.

Nearest Campground: McGee Creek Campground, at 7600 feet, has 30 fee sites for RVs and tents with flush toilets, drinking water, fire rings and shaded picnic tables. Some sites are reservable through www.recreation.gov or call 1-877-444-6777. Open May to October.

Lodging/Services: Mammoth Lakes has a wide variety of accommodations from moderate to pricey. Austria Hof Lodge 760-934-2764 is reasonably priced. Check AAA California Tour Book for other options in line with your budget.

Further Info: Inyo National Forest, White Mountain Ranger District 760-873-2500, 798 N. Main Street, Bishop, CA 93514. Backpackers should ask about wilderness permits.

User Groups: Hikers, horses and dogs, but no mountain bikes.

Hike Distance: 12 miles round trip to Steelhead Lake.

Difficulty: Strenuous.

Elevation: 8100 feet at trailhead, 10,400 feet at Steelhead Lake.

Best Times to Go: Midsummer to fall.

Cautions: Difficult stream crossings in early summer.

Other Maps: USGS 7.5-minute Convict Lake topo and/or *John Muir Wilderness, North Section.*

Other Attractions: Mammoth Lakes, an ever-spreading town in the woods, has a plethora of year-round services and recreational opportunities. McGee Creek Pack Station offers personalized vacations on horseback for individuals, families and groups, guided day rides, pack trips and mule-assisted support treks for hikers. Phone 760-935-4324 in summer, 760-878-2207 in winter. Website: www.mcgeecreekpackstation.com.

OF INTEREST

◆ McGee Creek Canyon features both one of Eastern Sierra's

loveliest wildflower displays and autumn color displays.

◆ Canyon offers gorgeous mountain landscapes with many subalpine and alpine lakes.

◆ Eastern gateway to Silver Divide country and other inner-Sierra destinations.

McGee Creek Trail enters John Muir Wilderness.

It isn't easy to pick the best season to hike in McGee Creek country. The first leg of the trail wanders through one of the Eastern Sierra's loveliest wildflower displays in early summer. By late September or early October, the ageless sorcery of autumn spreads over the canyon, igniting an explosion of color along the aspen-lined stream. Huge cottonwood and copper birch also join the fall foliage celebration.

Regardless of the season, this precipitous glacier-sculpted gash in Inyo National Forest contains marvelous scenery, showcasing some of the area's most beautiful mountain landscapes. Extraordinarily colorful canyon walls are striped like a stony parfait. The swirling bands of flashy hues are truly eye candy for High Country aficionados.

McGee Creek Trail leads to several subalpine and alpine lakes before crossing the Sierra Crest at 11,900 feet, 9 miles from the trailhead. The views from McGee Pass in a saddle between Red Slate Mountain and Red and White Mountain are stunning. To the west, hikers can gaze at Silver Divide at the head of wild and resplendent Fish Creek Valley. Eastward, the vista of the canyon you've just ascended is spectacular. The McGee route provides backpackers numerous inner-Sierra destinations beyond the pass.

To get your boots on the trail, turn off Highway 395 8.5 miles south of Mammoth Lakes junction (6.4 miles north of Tom's Place), and head west on McGee Creek Road. The arid, lackluster terrain is typical of most doorways to Eastern Sierra gorges. As a rule, they offer no hint of the grandeur hidden up-canyon. The 3.9-mile drive to the trailhead takes you past a campground and a pack station. A generous sample of McGee's charm begins the moment you exit the car at road's end. Views from the parking lot of the colorful environment are breathtaking, better than at the end of some hikes! Many natural features in the vicinity were named for the McGee brothers, Alney, Bart and

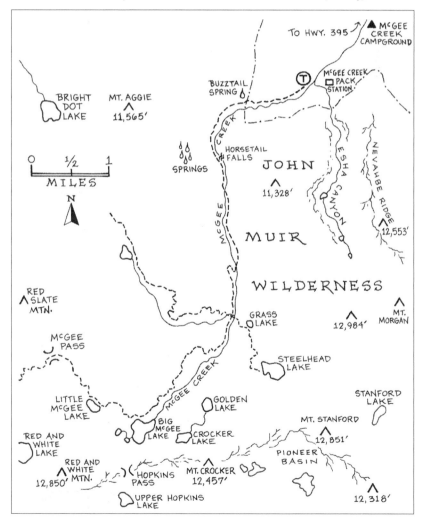

John, who were popular, respected pioneer homesteaders and cattlemen in Inyo and Mono Counties.

The turn off from Highway 395 marks a significant, but forgotten, remnant of Eastern Sierra skiing history. At the base of McGee Mountain, the area's first permanent rope tow hauled skiers up the slope. A piece of rusty machinery and a plaque mark the spot. The slope's gradient is tame by today's standards, but this was the place to ski in the 1930s and early 1940s.

Most races and events were held here because McGee had the only dependable rope tow, and its location next to the highway allowed easy access. In the early days of downhill skiing, most tows were small and portable so they could be moved easily to slopes where the snow was favorable. McGee Mountain also boasted an excellent ski school taught by soon-to-be-legendary Dave McCoy and others. Starting with a rope tow in 1941, McCoy was responsible for the development of skiing at Mammoth Mountain, now a nationally and internationally renowned winter sports destination.

Get an early start if you choose to hike during the dog days of August. Shade is in short supply for approximately the first 3 miles. Most will agree that it's less daunting to hike uphill in the cool of the day. Besides, the multicolored canyon walls are even more vibrant in early morning light. Just beyond the 8100-foot-elevation trailhead note a day use area, formerly a campground, set in a lush grove of rare copper birch, named for the color of its bark. Some of the largest aspen and birch on this side of the crest flourish next to the creek.

Ahead looms Red and White Mountain, flanked by Mounts Aggie, Baldwin, Crocker and Stanford. Except for Mount Aggie, elevation 11,565 feet, these dramatic peaks exceed 12,000 feet. Either walk along the creek on an old road that once served a campground or proceed uphill on the real trail that gradually climbs a sage-perfumed moraine. The creekside route joins the official trail in about a mile. In season, desert buckwheat and hundreds of thigh-high mule ears blanket the sandy slope. Their bright yellow flowers commingled with the watermelon-colored blooms of Indian paintbrush present a wonderfully gaudy picture. I suggest starting on the trail and ending the day along the creek. By late afternoon, you'll welcome the shade and a cooling foot bath.

Two whiskers shy of a mile, your route enters John Muir Wilderness. As you climb higher, the trail crosses seeps and side streams that host cheery wildflower gardens. A mile past aspen-shaded Buzztail Springs, feathery Horsetail Fall slithers down the canyon wall to the right. On the left, another slim, seasonal fall slides into McGee Creek. After the first crossing of McGee Creek, tricky when swollen with snow melt, the trail reaches a gorgeous meadow at 9055 feet around 3 miles. A short path leads down to it.

The stream-cut grassland provides a delightful niche to take a rest. Unac-

The trail approaches upper McGee Creek Canyon.

climated hikers or those seeking a shorter outing should consider this lovely spot a worthy destination. High Country meadows are fragile and easily destroyed. Remember that many mountain critters depend on this oasis for their survival. Be a thoughtful guest and leave no trace of your visit.

The trail narrows past the meadow and crosses McGee Creek on a log just above the ford. Be careful. This can be a difficult passage during peak run-off and/or if the log is unstable or missing. Before arriving at another junction, the trail bends around a sizable outcrop and cuts through a marshy stretch. Hikers will take great pleasure in this journey with constantly changing views, flowery meadows, colorful peaks and a spirited stream. Up to the Grass Lake/McGee Pass intersection around 3.7 miles, the route is actually a narrow, abandoned road constructed many years ago by owners of the Scheelore Tungsten Mine high above on the slope of Mount Baldwin. Each year the route looks more like a trail than a road.

If it's absolute solitude you're after, then heavenly Baldwin Canyon is where you need to be. But, you'll pay a price for it. It's a 2.5-mile-long, 1350-foot climb to Baldwin Lake, unnamed on maps, at 10,600 feet. The long defunct tungsten mine is a half-mile farther at 11,000 feet.

Our described route continues climbing along McGee Creek. Cross a tributary 0.7-mile past the right hand fork to the mine, and come to yet another junction. The right branch travels to McGee Lakes and McGee Pass, 5.8 miles distant, but you'll bear left for Grass Lake and Steelhead Lake. Again cross the creek and begin a zigzagging, 500-foot rise to a fork. Head left if you want to check out nearby meadow-ringed Grass Lake, elevation 9826 feet, at 4.5 miles. You'll find good rest spots and a few campsites at this pretty little lake. Otherwise, push on past the Grass Lake turnoff for 1.5 miles to reach Steelhead Lake. A few use trails established by anglers can be confusing. The main trail, however, generally travels southeast to Steelhead Lake at 6 miles from the parking area. You're faced with more steep switchbacks up to the beautiful 25-acre lake set in a rocky basin at 10,440 feet near timberline. En route, pause to let your heart catch up and drink in the superb High Country views.

At an unsigned intersection not indicated on maps, go left for Steelhead Lake. Shortly, you'll pass a tarn or two and descend briefly to the lake. Campsites are numerous. Find a comfortable place, break out the snacks or lunch and gape at the granite grandeur surrounding this sparkling alpine jewel. Choose a campsite if you're backpacking or return to the trailhead if you're a knapsacker. Don't forget to camp at least 100 feet (40 paces) away from the lake.

You might be tempted to visit the McGee Lakes or Pass while in the neighborhood, but keep in mind this is a vertical neighborhood. For those experienced in cross-country route finding, jaunts to Crocker Lake and Golden Lake are other possibilities. Study the map before you make a decision. The highly scenic extra mileage and elevation gain add up to a hefty day hike. Realistically assess your energy reserves, food and water supply and hours of remaining daylight to safely reach the trailhead before dark.

Rock Creek Canyon
Heavenly High Country and Pie in the Sky

◆ THE DETAILS

Getting There: From Highway 395 at Tom's Place, 15 miles south of Mammoth Lakes junction, turn west onto Rock Creek Road and drive 11 miles to road's end at Mosquito Flat Trailhead.

Nearest Campgrounds: Rock Creek Lake Campground has 28 sites, open June through September; East Fork, 3 miles down from the lake, opens in May and has 133 sites. There are also six other campgrounds in the lower canyon.

Lodging/Services: Rock Creek Lakes Resort 760-935-4311, Box 727, Bishop, CA 93515. Make reservations well in advance of your visit. They also have an excellent café. Showers are available at the café/store for a fee.

Further Info and Permits: Inyo National Forest, White Mountain Ranger District 760-935-2500.

User Groups: Hikers and equestrians. Dogs OK on leash.

Hike Distances: (all round trip) 4 miles to Long Lake, 5.4 miles to Chickenfoot Lake, 7.2 miles to Gem Lakes.

Difficulty: Easy to moderate.

Best Times to Go: Summer, early autumn.

Cautions: No campfires in Little Lakes Valley. This trail has a quota system for backpackers, permits necessary. Backpackers are required to use bear-resistant canisters in Little Lakes Valley, Morgan and Mono Passes.

Elevation: 10,255 feet at trailhead, 10,543 feet at Long Lake, 10,789 feet at Chickenfoot Lake, 10,880 feet at Gem Lakes.

Other Maps: Tom Harrison's ***Mono Divide High Country Trail Map***, or USGS Mount Tom, Mount Abbot 15-minute topos.

Winter Sports: Rock Creek Road is plowed in winter as far as the closed East Fork Campground. For a small fee payable at Tom's Place or Rock Creek Lodge, cross-country skiers and snowshoers can enjoy dramatic winter scenery. Rustic Rock Creek Lodge 877-935-4170, or www.rockcreeklodge.com, has small cabins, sauna, guided ski trips, and a dining room.

OF INTEREST

◆ The highest of all gateways into the Sierra Backcountry.

◆ Gentle basin with more than forty lakes offers abundant hiking choices, including many great and easy cross-country rambles.

◆ Heavenly pie and hearty food at Rock Creek Resort Café.

Among the high peaks surrounding Little Lakes Valley is Bear Creek Spire, elevation 13,713 feet.

While the Edenic beauty of all the Eastern Sierra's numerous canyons is extraordinary, Rock Creek's High Country landscape is particularly sensational. Sprawling below the granite ramparts of the Sierra Crest, it fairly gleams in the bright, wind-polished air. Surrounded by a brotherhood of 13,000-foot peaks, Little Lakes Valley sits in a broad, glacier-gouged trench webbed with merry streams and dazzling flowery meadows. At the head of the canyon, Mounts Mills, Dade, Abbot, Pyramid Peak and Bear Creek Spire impale the cobalt-blue sky, and jagged Wheeler Crest reigns on the skyline to the east.

Fabulous cloud sculptures often crown these bold, spiky summits that rise like gods above the horizon. Closer to earth, sunlight dances like quicksilver off dozens of lakes strung together like beads on a rosary. Besides offering the pleasures of full-blown, rampant summertime scenes, the canyon is a fantastic location to witness fall's pyrotechnics. Quaking aspens flaunt themselves like brazen hussies, celebrating the season in an orgy of shimmering colors.

One of the many enjoyable aspects of Little Lakes Valley is that it contains more than forty lakes, most of them off the beaten path but easily reached. Because the terrain is gentle, hikers are encouraged to abandon the primary route and explore these equally scenic but less visited lakes. This is an especially good plan during peak visitation on summer weekends.

Eleven miles of Rock Creek Canyon are open to automobiles. The remaining three miles through a basin, aptly called Little Lakes Valley, to the canyon headwall are designated wilderness, open only to pedestrians and equestrians. The paved road provides the highest gateway into Sierra backcountry, higher even than Tioga Pass or Whitney Portal. The drive alone paralleling lively Rock Creek in the midst of a rugged and lovely aspen-lined gorge is a stunner.

Climbing westward from Tom's Place on Highway 395, Rock Creek Road first winds by the muted hues of sagebrush and piñon pine-studded slopes. As the road gains altitude, drab tones are soon replaced by the lush greenery of early summer or the fiery, autumn-kissed colors of aspen, birch, cottonwood and willow. Meandering past enticing creekside campsites, two small resorts, Rock Creek Lake and a pack station, the scenic byway ends at lofty Mosquito Flat Trailhead, elevation 10,255 feet, a little more than a mile beyond the lake.

Although you don't have to get out of the car to appreciate this consummate alpine setting, the best is yet to come if you let your feet lead the way. Fortunately, by the time you arrive at the trailhead, your vehicle has done most of the climbing. You'll soon realize that you don't have to stroll far to reap the rewards for abandoning the family flivver.

The suggested hike follows what was once a busy road to a major mining location in the next canyon south. The road from Tom's Place that penetrates Rock Creek Canyon turns south at Mosquito Flat, crosses Morgan Pass and continues to the now defunct Pine Creek Tungsten Mine and Mill. This was the operation's primary corridor route from the mid-1920s to the 1940s. Before this sublime environment was protected as John Muir Wilderness, a constant stream of growling ore trucks shattered the valley's tranquility and profoundly marred its grandeur. During World War II, a road was built directly up Pine Creek Canyon to make access to the nation's largest tungsten mine at 11,000 feet less difficult during winter. The Morgan Pass Road through Rock Creek Canyon was permanently closed at Mosquito Flat in the 1950s.

I must confess that besides world-class scenery, another reason I'm drawn to Little Lakes Valley is the homemade pie at Rock Creek Lakes Resort Café. God forbid if I seem to trivialize such a convocation of natural wonders by touting something so mundane, but Sue King, resident Pastry Maven, gives a whole new meaning to "pie in the sky." Après hike, devouring a generous hunk of, say, key lime pie, at 10,000 feet is in itself a slice of heaven not to be missed if you are anywhere within striking distance of this canyon. Since 1979 the King family has owned and operated the business which started in 1923 in a one-room store that mainly sold fishing tackle for 30 years.

Experiencing Rock Creek Canyon's glorious terrain reinforces the importance and urgency of preserving other stunning ecosystems, home to an intricate, interdependent network of wildlife and plants. Saving what little remains of these wild landscapes is one of the biggest challenges facing us in

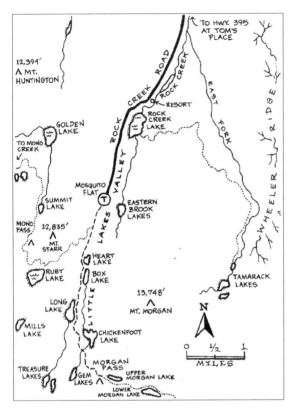

the twenty-first century. John Muir Wilderness protects 580,675 acres, the third largest of eighteen designated wilderness areas in the Sierra Nevada. The Wilderness Act of 1964 represented a landmark piece of environmental legislation, setting aside precious ecoregions "where earth and its community of life remain untrammeled, where man is a visitor who does not remain."

THE HIKE

A delightful 3.6-mile hike to Gem Lakes at the headwall below Morgan Pass begins at the end of Mosquito Flat parking area. Bear in mind as you ramble in the midst of overwhelmingly striking scenery, it simply doesn't matter how far you roam today. One-half mile, ten miles, it's all beautiful. Remember the old cliché—it's the journey, not the destination.

At 0.3 mile the trail enters John Muir Wilderness and makes a brief, moderate ascent of Crankcase Grade, the name of which suggests its former usage. For the next 3 miles there is but a modest elevation gain until the switchbacks below 11,155-foot Morgan Pass. Rest assured that this is not a slog-and-pant expedition only for strapping Sierra trompers. If you walk no farther than 0.5 mile to a fantastic viewpoint atop a little rise just before the Mono Pass trail junction, you'll have a glorious picture of what classic Eastern Sierra High Country is all about.

Stay left at the junction and continue on the gentle trail toward Morgan Pass. You'll first pass Mack Lake, hard to see in the gully below unless you're looking for it. As you travel on, the trail passes through colorful alpine flower gardens, brilliantly green meadows and by a succession of lovely lakes and ponds. Each lake is a scenic destination to while away the day. Reach Marsh

Lake at one mile, followed by Heart Lake and large Box Lake around 1.7 miles. Just to the east beyond this string of lakes lies another cluster of watery gems, all within an easy, off-trail, 0.5-mile walk. In all, close to fifty lakes are within a two-hour walk or horseback ride from the trailhead.

The trail skirts the east shore of deep Long Lake, perhaps the most charming of the lakes. It's a great spot for a snack break. Relax on one of the many lakeside rocks and allow the magic of this extraordinary setting to fill your senses. Directly across the lake, numerous colorfully banded peaks challenge the skyline. Walk on the nearly level, flower-lined trail to the end of Long Lake before beginning a gradual 0.7-mile ascent to the Chickenfoot Lake spur, unmarked on maps, at 2.7 miles. Turn left and walk five minutes to the shore of ravishing Chickenfoot Lake, 10,789 feet, and its breathtaking panorama of Little Lakes Valley.

If you opt to bypass Chickenfoot, walk 0.3 mile uphill past the unsigned spur, descend to and cross Gem Lakes' outlet stream. A sign points left to Morgan Pass and right to Gem Lakes. Bear right to reach the lakes. The first two are more like ponds, while the last and highest hunkering below a cliff is the largest. A use trail heads west to high and wild Treasure Lakes, elevation 11,200 feet. Backpackers take note that either Gem or Treasure Lakes is ideal for a base camp to investigate Rock Creek headwaters and explore the Morgan Pass environs. In all, you've only gained 550 feet of elevation between here and the trailhead, a very minimal amount relative to most Eastern Sierra canyon trails. When you can tear yourself away from upper Rock

Peaks and granite surround Rock Creek Lake.

Creek's spell, return the way you came and enjoy the landscape again from a different perspective.

It will be obvious that the farther you travel away from the parking area, the fewer people you'll see. In addition to the main trail through Little Lakes Valley, check the map for other destinations that branch off of it. Strenuous trips to Hilton Lakes and Mono Pass are described in Chapters 23 and 24. A moderately strenuous trail to a clutch of lakes east of Rock Creek Lake leads to Kenneth, Francis, Dorothy and Tamarack Lakes, between two and five miles distant at the base of massive, sheer-faced Wheeler Ridge.

Box Lake in Little Lakes Valley

Hilton Creek Canyon
A Perfect 10

◆ THE DETAILS

Getting There: To find the trailhead, follow directions to Rock Creek in Chapter 22.

Nearest Campground: See Chapter 22.

Lodging: See Chapter 22.

Further Info and Permits: Inyo National Forest 760-873-2500, permits 760-873-2483, 351 Pacu Lane, Suite 200, Bishop, CA 95314.

User Groups: Hikers and horses. Dogs OK on leash.

Hike Distance: 9 miles round trip to Hilton 2 Lake, 10 miles round trip to Davis Lake, 8.75 miles round trip to Hilton 3 Lake, 9.75 miles round trip to Hilton 4 Lake, various mileages to upper lakes.

Difficulty: Moderately strenuous to Hilton 2 or Davis Lake, strenuous to Hilton 3 and beyond.

Best Times to Go: Midsummer through early October.

Cautions: No campfires above 10,000 feet. Fires OK at Hilton 2 and Davis Lakes. Backpackers should store food in bear-resistant canisters.

Elevation: 9860 feet at trailhead. 9852 feet at Hilton 2, 9808 feet at Davis Lake, 10,300 feet at Hilton 3, 10,353 feet at Hilton 4, up to 11,150 feet for Hilton Lakes 5 through 10.

Other Maps: **John Muir Wilderness Map**, Tom Harrison's **Mono Divide High Country Trail Map**, USGS Mount Abbot and Mount Morgan 15-minute topos.

OF INTEREST

◆ Ten serene lakes in a rugged, glacier-carved canyon.

◆ Impressive wildflower displays.

◆ Head of canyon nestles beneath immense 12,000-foot-plus peaks.

A trail over the divide west of Rock Creek Canyon leads to a group of beautiful lakes below Mount Stanford and Mount Huntington in John Muir Wilderness. A hike to one or more of them is perfect for a day trip or a three-day backpack. Ten serene, sun-splashed lakes are scattered along Hilton Creek in a rugged glacier-gouged canyon. Ranging in elevation between 9808 feet and

11,150 feet, the staircase lakes vary significantly in size and character. Half-mile-long Hilton 1, more commonly known as Davis Lake, is the largest.

At a junction 4 miles from the trailhead, you'll need to decide which of the lakes will be your destination. Both Davis and Hilton 2 are handsome, forest-fringed, high elevation lakes. However, Hilton 2's setting is deemed by some to be more dramatic, while Davis' surprisingly warm water and little sandy beaches appeal to others. Both are popular with backpackers, and both are large enough to afford privacy.

For more seclusion, pitch your tent at Hilton Lake 3 or 4. Remember, no campfires are allowed above 10,000 feet. The lakes are smaller the farther you travel up-canyon, and Hilton Lakes 6 through 10 are alpine puddles, comparatively. Hilton Lake 10, highest and most remote, sits in a stark cup at the end of the canyon beneath 12,394-foot Mount Huntington.

To find the trailhead, follow directions to Rock Creek in Chapter 22. How-

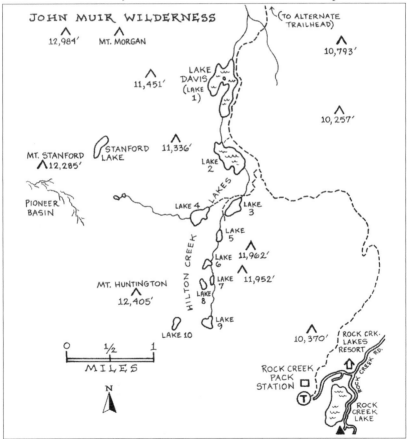

ever, you'll find the Hilton Canyon Trailhead 9.2 miles from the highway just before you reach the pack station well before road's end. Watch for trailhead parking near the Hilton-Davis sign. Here and at all Eastern Sierra trailheads, do not leave food or scented items in your vehicle. Covering up a cooler or placing it in the trunk will not keep a bear out of your car for more than thirty seconds. Their sense of smell is off-the-charts acute. Do your part to keep these always-hungry bruins wild by making sure food and other fragrant things are unavailable to them. Under current wilderness management policies, if a bear damages your property to get your food, it is your fault. The bear is just being a bear, but you can be fined for improper food storage.

If you're interested in having the trail all to yourself, try another route into Hilton Lakes. This one dates back to the early 1900s and was in use before the trail from Rock Creek Lake. This lonely path starts near aspen-lined Hilton Creek in the wee community of Crowley Lake. Adding to its anonymity, the trailhead is neither obvious from the paved road nor signed. However, it's not hard to locate with map in hand. Although nothing remains, the area was the site of a very popular rustic lodge and pack station until 1962. A few natural features in the vicinity are namesakes of Long Valley rancher Richard

Hilton Lake #3

Hilton. In the 1870s he owned a dairy operation in the lush grasslands near what is now Hilton Creek. Mrs. Hilton was locally a well-known midwife.

If you choose this essentially unknown access to Hilton Canyon, you should be aware of the tradeoffs. The route is unmaintained and rarely used because it begins at a much lower elevation than the Rock Creek trailhead. You'll immediately be faced with a hot, 1600-foot climb up a brushy high desert moraine and then a 1000-foot ascent to Davis Lake. This is a long, tough trip for unconditioned hikers, especially if laden with a heavy pack. But, if you're a lonely-and-lovin'-it trekker, this trail is for you. Note that the parking area indicated on the John Muir Wilderness map is now much closer to the road, and the BLM campground has been abandoned for years.

To those of you who have racked up a number of Eastern Sierra hikes, Hilton Lakes Trail is not likely to ring the bell on your hike-o-meter. Although the lake-dotted basin is dramatically beautiful, the journey to it is not particularly scenic. Views are brief and limited. The undulating path ultimately rises 500 feet, tops the ridge separating Hilton and Rock Creeks, drops into Hilton Canyon and intersects the Hilton Creek Trail. The dusty, roller-coaster route travels over sandy, exposed slopes and through forest cover en route to the divide at 10,380 feet.

In season, impressive wildflower displays brighten the sunny, open slopes. Pass through an area of uprooted trees mowed down by an avalanche in the 1980s. Begin a steep, zigzagging descent into Hilton Canyon at 3.7 miles. Rest your knees for a moment when you catch a glimpse of distant Davis Lake peeking through the forest. Reach a junction at 4 miles and choose your destination. A sign announces that right (north) takes you down to Hilton 2 and Davis Lake (Hilton 1), and left (southwest) leads to Hilton Lakes 3 through 6.

Hikers or backpackers heading for Hilton 2 need to turn left at an unmarked fork 0.5 mile past the signed intersection. You'll soon reach stunning, forest-ringed Hilton 2. Mount Huntington, elevation 12,405 feet, presides over the southwest end of the lake. Numerous excellent campsites can be found on the lake's east side as well as across the outlet at the north end.

Hilton 2 has a lingering aura of history about it, and you might find bits of it on the northeast side. The best preserved remnant is a log jam at the outlet stream. Hand-cut and notched, the logs were obviously once part of a structure. For decades Hilton Lake 2 was the site of a rustic fishing camp. The first of three owners was named Brown who in the 1920s was granted a 99-year lease by the Forest Service. Brown's Camp consisted of a cook shack, corral and fourteen small log cabins. The Pearson family bought it in 1946, but this time Inyo National Forest mandated that at the end of fifteen years every sign of human occupation had to be removed to allow the site to revert to its natural state.

The industrious Pearsons made extensive improvements and catered to a high-end clientele who returned year after year to the same housekeeping cabins. Guests and everything else, including twelve-foot-long rowboats for lakes 1 through 4, were packed in on horses and mules from "Lower Camp" along Hilton Creek 2600 feet below. Lower Camp was headquarters for the

Mount Huntington towers above Hilton Lake #4.

pack operation. A few rooms were available there for clients who wanted to rest the night before the six-mile ride.

With just three years left on the lease, Pearson sold the successful seasonal business in early 1959 to a man named Kyte. Kyte, for some reason, believed he could persuade the Forest Service to extend the lease. However, the

Wilderness Act was on the horizon, and the Forest Service declined to grant him an extension. In 1962 officials told Kyte that everything in "Upper Camp" had to be removed, leaving no trace of human tenancy around the lakeshore. Rumor has it that rather than packing out a mountain of equipment, he instead dumped everything in the deep end of the lake. Except for a dozen or so logs bobbing in the shallows at the outlet, charred bits of wood suggest the structures were probably burned.

If you're bound for Davis Lake, 0.5-mile distant, bear right at the unsigned "Y" and then right again at another unmarked fork. The path from the second fork will take you to the west side of Davis Lake. Good campsites can be found among the lodge pole pines at the head of the lake.

To experience the canyon's true alpine charms, aim for Hilton Lakes 3 through 10 by turning left at the signed junction. Hilton 3 is only 0.4 mile away. Hop over a seasonal creek and pass a wee meadow before grunting up a short set of really steep switchbacks. Take a breather at the top and enjoy a marvelous view of Hilton 2, Davis Lake and Glass Mountain Ridge in the distance. It's a quick stroll to Lake 3's flowery shoreline and knockout setting dominated by majestic Mount Huntington and Mount Stanford in the background. Use trails lead to limited camping on the southeast side. A few others overlook the lake on the northwest side.

Stay on the main trail for 0.5 mile to reach Lake 4. Cross Hilton 3's outlet, continue along the northwest shoreline and cross a little ridge offering a tantalizing shot of Hilton 5's outlet cascade. The trail dips a bit to a verdant meadow, pops up over a low ridge and reaches Hilton 4, elevation 10,353 feet, at nearly 5 miles from the trailhead. Mount Huntington is the dramatic peak on the opposite side of the lake. After a long lunch break and perhaps a chilly swim, retrace your footsteps back to Rock Creek Trailhead.

Camping at either spectacular Hilton 3 or 4 puts you in good position for a leisurely day hike to the wildly beautiful, alpine world of Hilton Lakes 5 through 10. Although the topo shows one, there is no trail leading from Lake 3 to the higher lakes. However, a short scramble up the rocky west end will soon get you to Lake 5. To continue the scenic, high elevation journey to the lakes in upper Hilton Canyon, you'll essentially be tracing their outlet streams. Lake 10 is the most isolated and sits off by itself to the west at the head of the glacial amphitheater. Distance between lakes ranges from approximately 0.25 to 0.5 mile.

A very well-conditioned, acclimated hiker could complete the trip to the upper lakes and back in a day. But, if like me, you place more value on the journey than the destination, then camp overnight at Lake 3 or 4. Doing so affords you a leisurely and more intimate exploration of Hilton Canyon's sublime landscape and brilliant gemlike lakes.

24
Mosquito Flat to Mono Pass
A High Octane Hike

◆ THE DETAILS

Except items below, same as for Rock Creek Canyon, Chapter 22.

Further Info and Permits: Inyo National Forest 760-873-2500, permits 760-873-2483, 351 Pacu Lane, Suite 200, Bishop, CA 93514.

Hike Distance: 4.5 miles round trip to Ruby Lake, 7.4 miles round trip to Mono Pass, 8.4 miles round trip to Mount Starr's summit.

Cautions: Bear-resistant canisters are recommended for all wilderness areas, but backpackers are required to use them in Little Lakes Valley, Morgan and Mono Passes.

Map: See page 160.

OF INTEREST

◆ The highest of all gateways into the Sierra Backcountry.

◆ Eastern gateway to the spectacularly glaciated Mono Recesses.

◆ Possibly the most dazzling alpine wildflower display in the Eastern Sierra.

◆ Described hike leads to sweeping vistas of a vast chunk of the High Sierra both east and west of the Sierra Crest.

◆ Don't forget the to-die-for pie at Rock Creek Lakes Resort.

The strenuous hike to Mono Pass begins at Mosquito Flat, the highest trailhead in the Sierra at 10,250 feet. Don't confuse this Mono Pass with the other one on the eastern boundary of Yosemite National Park slightly south of Tioga Pass. This 3.7-mile jaunt to the Sierra Crest on the boundary of Sierra and Inyo National Forests is one of several memorable trails out of Rock Creek Canyon.

Rock Creek is one of the range's largest glacial troughs and home to more than forty lakes (see Chapter 22). Only a half-day hike away, many more High Country lakes are accessible over Morgan and Mono Passes. Thanks to a high starting point, knapsackers and backpackers can reach alpine backcountry with less climbing than from other trailheads. The extraordinary trip to Mono Pass should be on every hiker's "must do" list.

If this outing marks your debut into Eastern Sierra canyons, the nonstop scenery may very well establish the benchmark by which you judge other canyons. The huge, deep gorge contains an astounding convocation of natural features that often render visitors popeyed with wonder. In the upper reaches of Rock Creek Canyon, lush Little Lakes Valley sprawls beneath a granite wall of 13,000-foot peaks dominated by magnificent Bear Creek Spire. Studded with clusters of lakes, large and small, verdant stream-cut meadows host perhaps the most dazzling alpine wildflower gardens in the Eastern Sierra. In autumn the landscape turns to gold as grasses, willows and thousands of aspens put on their season finale.

Many visitors believe Rock Creek to be nature's most eloquent example of canyon scenery. It is indeed a masterpiece of creation, but then all Eastern Sierra canyons are masterpieces. Despite similar origins and geomorphology, each has its unique personality and moods. All of the magnificent gorges have enormous sensory appeal. In my view, only the undiscerning or novice canyon traveler would try to rank them. Doing so would be akin to comparing a succulent peach to a tangy, tart apple. Although each one has a different texture and taste, both are delicious.

Begin your journey at the end of a large, paved parking area. As you can tell from the number of cars, Rock Creek Canyon is a Mecca for hikers, especially on weekends in July and August. The gentle elevation rise through the incomparable sights of Little Lakes Valley makes it a very popular destination for hikers of all abilities and ages. If possible, plan your visit on weekdays. However, you'll only be on the main trail for a few minutes. At 0.6 mile, bear right at the junction signed for Mono Pass.

Rocky switchbacks traverse several benches, moving you sharply uphill through scattered lodge pole and whitebark pines. Shortly, a spur from the pack station merges with your route. Remember to always give horses and mules the right-of-way, stopping off the trail if possible to let them pass. Please don't spook them. The trail is very steep, narrow and has dangerous drop-offs. A steady climb reveals increasingly expansive views of sublime Little Lakes Valley. Each uphill step offers more spectacular scenery. Keeping your eyes on the trail rather than glued to the inexhaustible scenery is one of the challenges of this hike.

Pass an attractive little tarn around 1.5 miles. The grade intensifies and then mellows out a bit in a meadow near a junction to unseen Ruby Lake at 2 miles. If you take this spur, 0.25-mile climb along the outlet brings you to Ruby, elevation 11,100 feet, a stunning watery gem set in a drop-dead gorgeous, granite cirque topped by spiky pinnacles. Try not to miss this alpine beauty. Unconditioned visitors may want to make this their destination, and backpackers may consider setting up camp in the vicinity of the outlet. Don't forget to camp at least 40 paces away from the water. No campfires are allowed at this elevation.

If you choose to bypass the short detour to Ruby, then get your body in four-wheel drive and attack the remaining 1.7 miles to Mono Pass. As you proceed up the north wall of the cirque, the zigzagging ascent really kicks in. Mono Pass is only 1000 feet above, but as you struggle upward, it may feel like 10,000 feet. En route, deep, blue Ruby Lake comes into view.

Ruby Lake from the trail to Mono Pass

The view into Rock Creek Canyon from the Mono Pass Trail

Backdropped by the Sierra Crest's formidable crags, the vista is guaranteed to take your breath away, assuming you have any left! This environment is the no frills essence of the Sierra Nevada: buck-naked stone beneath a cobalt blue sky, a landscape virtually unchanged since its creation.

It's a world of clean, gleaming, fractured granite, acres and acres of it. Austere takes on new meaning in this setting. Other locales I've described as austere or stark seem almost lush by comparison. There is a raw, primeval energy in these high, wild places that becomes more compelling and comfortable—and addicting—with every visit. Up here you can feel the very bones of the Sierra beneath your boots. No doubt, such settings rouse a slumbering gene that sequesters our dormant wild side.

The relentless ascent takes you through a shallow gully before the final push to 12,045-foot Mono Pass. By the time you reach the top, you'll probably be gasping for air and thinking someone must have snuck bowling balls in your pack. Take a break, and after your heart stops doing the Macarena, give some thought to three options available from here. Views from the narrow pass straddling the Inyo-Fresno County line are good, but you can do better. Much better, in fact.

To the left of the sign, a faint path cuts uphill for .25 mile to an unbelievable vista. Find a soft rock and feast on sweeping views of the Mono Recesses, the jewel-like lakes in Pioneer Basin and several snowcapped peaks. Native

Americans used the pass for centuries as a trading route, and the scenery, as they saw it, hasn't changed. The first non-indigenous people to explore the area were members of the 1864 California Geological Survey. They followed the old Indian trail over the crest and camped far below along Mono Creek before moving west into Yosemite.

Another option is to descend the sandy trail to stark little Summit Lake. It's a half-mile drop to its placid, steely-blue waters at 11,190 feet. Downhill may sound appealing at this point, but remember it's a 900-foot uphill grind back to the pass. Furthermore, you'll have all the downhill you can handle on the return to Mosquito Flat. Some will find the extra mileage to the lake a thoroughly masochistic exercise. Others, however, will enjoy the extra mileage to Summit Lake's rockbound, alpine setting.

For a quintessential experience in this magnificent section of the Sierra, hikers with energy to burn are strongly encouraged to scramble up to the summit of Mount Starr, a half mile northeast of the pass. It's a relatively easy, but steep, Class 2 maneuver up the west slope to the 12,835-foot summit. The 800-foot gain is steep, but it is not scary or exposed. The 360-degree panorama from the broad, sandy summit is, to use the word appropriately, awesome.

It seems as if you have the entire world at your feet. Peaks, mountains, valleys and ridges melt into the horizon. On top of this stunning aerie, find wind

Along the Mono Pass Trail

as free and bold as an eagle, beauty so great your heart will race and quiet so deep you can hear the pulse of the Sierra. Chances are good that you'll never get to Mount Everest, but the intoxicating view from Mount Starr will give you an idea of why climbers do what they do, what they live for. Study the map for place names too numerous to identify here.

Walter Starr, prominent San Franciscan and early Sierra Club member, in 1896 was the first to stand on top of the mountain. His son, Walter (Pete) Starr, Jr., was a formidable hiker, a la John Muir, and an icon in the climbing world by age 30. Tragically, in 1933, his life ended among the Sierra peaks where he felt truly alive. Legendary climber Norman Clyde found Starr's body where he'd fallen on Michael Minaret. On a 12,000-foot ledge, his remains were carefully covered with rocks to rest for eternity in the mountains that he loved.

When you've had your fill of the heavenly scenery, return the way you came. You'll agree that the terrain is just as mesmerizing on the way down. Watch your step, especially if you're tired and your legs feel a bit wobbly. It's wise to be off this steep, rocky trail before daylight fades.

Lower Pine Lake in Pine Creek Canyon

Pine Creek Canyon
Diabolically Steep Portal to Heavenly Scenery

◆ THE DETAILS

Getting There: From Bishop, drive 10 miles north on Highway 395 and turn west (left) onto Pine Creek/Rovana Road. (From the north, drive 28 miles south from Mammoth Junction to the Pine Creek Road turnoff.) Drive 9.5 miles to road's end and park. Walk behind the corral to gain the trail.

Nearest Campground: Some primitive, no fee sites are along the creek on the left just before the pack station.

Lodging/Services: Bishop is a full service town. Try Bishop Days Inn 760-872-1095.

Further Info: Inyo National Forest 760-873-2500.

User Groups: Hikers and equestrians. Dogs OK on leash east of Sierra Crest.

Hike Distance: 9 miles round trip to Lower Pine Lake.

Difficulty: Very strenuous.

Best Times to Go: Summer, autumn.

Cautions: No campfires above 10,000 feet.

Elevation: 7400 feet at trailhead, 9942 feet at Lower Pine Lake.

Other Maps: USGS Mount Tom 7.5-minute topo, Inyo National Forest Map for overview.

Trip Note: If you want to base camp at one of the lakes in the upper canyon or beyond but don't want to schlep a heavy backpack, contact Pine Creek Pack Station 760-387-2797. For a reasonable fee, they'll drop you off you at a destination of your choice.

OF INTEREST

◆ Multicolored peaks accentuate the beauty of this precipitous canyon.

◆ Truly gargantuan in scale.

◆ Difficult but little-used route into Kings Canyon Park High Country.

Numerous glacier-scoured canyons along the Eastern Sierra escarpment between Bridgeport and Lone Pine safeguard some of the West's most sensational scenery. Because entrances to these great gashes are unremarkable and offer no hint of the splendor they hold, their beauty comes as a surprise, making the dramatic landscape even more awe-inspiring.

Essentially, the U-shaped canyons share many similar features: deep, steep-sided valleys, lush and flowery meadows, chain lakes, sparkling streams, arc-shaped moraines, sky-high peaks, coniferous forests and stands of elegant aspen that light up the scenery with brilliant colors in autumn.

Despite being created by essentially the same geologic forces, each Sierra canyon has its own distinct character and unique grandeur. In a sense, they are

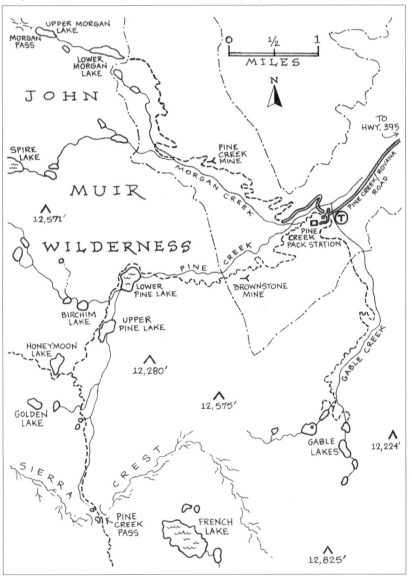

like siblings. Each one is different but you can see the family resemblance. Their nuances grow with familiarity as one becomes better acquainted. Weather, season and time of day also influence their singular qualities.

Like its neighboring canyons, Pine Creek, 19 miles northwest of Bishop, bestows visual euphoria to all who enter. After turning off Highway 395 onto Pine Creek/Rovana Road, it's 9.5 miles to the end of the road. As you near the tiny settlement of Rovana, it will be obvious that you're about to witness a masterpiece of glacial power. Ahead, rocky and barren peaks gnaw at the sky, promising visitors strenuous hiking in spectacular High Country.

The byway parallels Pine Creek as it passes between two long lateral moraines left by the union of glaciers from Gable Creek, Morgan Creek and upper Pine Creek. The road ends in a forested area at a pack station, trailhead parking and a gate blocking motorized access to a defunct tungsten mine. Besides their immensity and height, colorful mountains set against a peacock-blue sky provide a jaw-dropping sight. The sheer peaks sport colors you would think impossible on stark hunks of rock.

Several challenging options await you from the trailhead, but the 4.5-mile trek to Lower Pine Lake is an excellent choice for day-trippers and hardy backpackers to sample the canyon's rugged grandeur. Let it be known that the start of this journey is wickedly steep, gaining 2000 feet in 2.5 miles. The remaining two miles are just doggone steep. Beginning in a mixed forest behind the pack station, the trail crosses several creeklets decorated with wild rose, tiger lily, columbine, monkshood and Queen Anne's lace.

All too soon the trail leaves the forest's shady sanctuary as you huff and puff ever upward. Directly across the narrow canyon, the carcass of a bygone tungsten mill scars the mountainside. Thankfully, it is soon out of sight. In spite of this brief intrusion at the beginning, the vistas are breathtaking. Over-the-shoulder views draw the eye across Owens Valley far below, revealing the vast volcanic tablelands and White Mountains.

Take a breather and ponder the existence of Pine Creek Mine in this stunning Sierra location. It was once the major tungsten producer in America, as well as one of the largest tungsten (scheelite) deposits in the world. Although tungsten was discovered in 1913, Pine Creek didn't begin full-scale operations until 1938 when World War II was on the horizon. Due to its extraordinarily high melting point, 6170 degrees Fahrenheit, tungsten was of vital importance in the manufacture of heat-resistant steel and other products ranging from wire filaments to armor-piercing projectiles.

Owned by Union Carbide for most of its productive years, it operated round-the-clock year-round for 53 years. Cutting edge technology developed at Pine Creek thrust it into the vanguard of the tungsten mining industry. During its heyday, 400 miners, geologists, engineers, truck drivers and office personnel were employed. Everyone lived in the company town of Rovana.

Looking down Pine Creek Canyon to the abandoned mine, with Owens Valley and White Mountains beyond

Daily, regardless of weather, employees were bused to and from work. As important as Pine Creek was to the nation's defense needs, it was also a big factor in the local economy.

By 1991 the "Mine in the Sky," as it was called, could no longer compete with China, a nation rich in tungsten and even richer in cheap labor. During its last five years of life, the mine was quiet, but the mill was busy processing imported ore from China. At present, the extensive facility is being cleaned up, dismantled and hauled away to comply with state and federal environmental laws.

Today, the mine that for decades coaxed tungsten from the belly of the mountain is peaceful, but its footprint in this otherwise pristine environment is still evident. One can only imagine the din from a parade of ore trucks growling up and down the canyon, equipment racket and the endless tram circuit of ore buckets between mine and mill. It is anticipated, however, that in time the area will revert to its natural state. Let's hope so.

After a rest, continue your vertical saunter on the exposed, steep trail. Around 1.1 miles, join the rough and rocky remains of a road carved out of the slope to reach Brownstone (tungsten) Mine, operational in 1952-53. The road zigzags uphill in long, punishing switchbacks. The good news is that the canyon's rugged, knockout scenery improves with every step. Its rocky architecture and classic glacial features are spellbinding. You'll also note that day hikers are scarce, probably because of the precipitous grade and remote trailhead.

The ascent relaxes briefly at a creek crossing at 1.5 miles. Put your legs in low gear and start climbing again, marveling at stubby Sierra junipers along the way. Some of the snags have weathered to a lovely nutmeg-colored hue. As the route bends left toward the abandoned mine, trade the rocky road for a rocky trail and more switchbacks. At the junction, look for a filled-in adit, tramway cables and barricaded openings in the rock wall above. Sections of the trail have been "improved" with uncomfortably tall steps which are difficult to negotiate in either direction, especially if carrying a 40-pound backpack.

The trail fords another nameless creek and switchbacks up to a sign announcing John Muir Wilderness at approximately 3.5 miles. By now you most likely will have shot a roll of film to memorialize the canyon's grandeur. At the boundary the path swings north and soon reaches the end of the worst of this grueling climb. The grade eases as you proceed through thin forest cover to the welcome tune of nearby Pine Creek. At 4.2 miles the trail dips and parallels the tumbling stream for the remaining 0.3 mile to Lower Pine Lake.

Unload your pack and tarry along the charming waterway for awhile. Diminutive waterfalls and dozens of toe-tempting pools are a refreshing reward for pooped hikers. After cooling off, make your way to 16-acre Lower Pine Lake at 9942 feet. At the unsigned fork, 4.5 miles from the trailhead, bear left to excellent campsites not far from the lake's northeast shore. You can absorb the magnificent alpine ambiance here from many choice places.

Bear right at the fork, cross a log bridge and shortly pass through a drift fence to access the rockbound northwest shore. An absolutely awesome mountain of stone rules the terrain above Lower Pine Lake. From its summit to its base, it is striated with black, pink and white bands. If you have energy left, continue walking a moderate grade to Upper Pine Lake at 10,230 feet. It's another watery alpine jewel that invites lingering.

When it's time, retrace your steps. The return trip is certainly not aerobically challenging, but it's just as steep as the ascent. Tighten boot laces to prevent jammed toes. Be careful, especially if you're tired, descending the tall steps that must have been designed for a giant. Don't be in a rush to leave this fantastic high-elevation world. Stop often to imprint this special place in your heart.

Eastern Sierra canyons are renowned for their steepness, some more than others, but the payoff for sojourners is priceless. Said a hiker in the 1920s, "Let us remember that there will always be those who know that the most marvelous views are seen only after physical effort to obtain them."

About Bighorn Sheep:
Bravest of all Mountaineers

I've been privileged to observe many species of Sierra wildlife while on hikes and backpacks, but a bighorn sheep is the one critter I'd give my first born to see. So far, these majestic animals have remained elusive, but I don't take it personally. Even John Muir, greatest of all Sierra wanderers, only saw bighorns once in all of his rambles in High Country.

Frankly, a sighting of an alien spacecraft above timberline is more likely than catching a glimpse of a bighorn or two in the Sierra. After all, they do hang out in lofty elevations in the air that angels breathe where two leggeds infrequently intrude. More relevant, only about 400 Sierra bighorns exist as of 2009, and sightings are extremely rare. These splendid mountain monarchs are rarer than the Florida panther and California condor. They are clearly one of the most endangered mammals in North America.

John Muir regarded bighorns, Ovis canadensis as the "bravest of Sierra mountaineers." Indeed, they are the quintessential symbol of High Sierra wilderness, reminding us of an era when their mountain realm was vastly less accessible and altered by modern humans. Their rugged character matches the austere above tree line habitat they call home. Recent research says that they are a genetically distinct subspecies of desert bighorns that evolved in only the eastern portion of the southern and central Sierra. These animals have long survived in alpine landscapes of sparse vegetation and wicked winters.

Dr. John Wehausen, pre-eminent wild sheep researcher, said "were granite to come alive, it would undoubtedly look like a bighorn sheep, so perfectly do they blend into the landscape." They are so integral to their environment they look like rocks with legs. Bighorns are stocky and short-legged, but they move with amazing grace and agility in their vertical stony world. Burly builds and short legs, however, prevent the speed necessary to outrun predators.

Bighorns utilize rocky steep slopes along the Sierra Crest for safety from predators, bedding down on seemingly inaccessible ledges at night. While feeding they stay near more rugged terrain and cliffs should they need to scramble to safety. The primary sense used to detect predators is very keen eyesight, and their optimal habitat is visually wide open where trespassers can be spotted at long distances. In summer, Sierra wild sheep roam along the stark crest between 10,000-14,000 feet. Although they are capable of remaining at high elevations in winter, they prefer to live at the foot of the eastern Sierra escarpment where climatic conditions are less severe and the forage more nutritious and plentiful.

Before the invasion of Euro-Americans during the Gold Rush, bighorns occurred in scattered herds along the entire Sierra crest and the Great Western Divide. Since then things have never been the same for wild sheep whose survival depends on a fragile, undisturbed, intact ecosystem. Healthy domestic sheep carry bacteria that almost always cause fatal pneumonia in bighorns if contact occurs. Lower altitude habitat disruption and domestic sheep encounters are the primary factors explaining much of their historic decline beginning in the mid-1800s.

From twenty wild sheep herds numbering well over a thousand, their population plummeted to the hundreds. In 1878 state law gave Sierra bighorns full protection from hunting, which is still in effect. Nonetheless, for the next century wild sheep continued to disappear. But the 1970s only 250 sheep remained. Despite a hunting ban, bighorns teetered on the brink of extinction.

Between 1979-88 wildlife biologists split up the population and used the remaining sheep to reestablish three additional herds in other Sierra locations. Initially, the cooperative state and federal program effected a reversal of the decline, increasing the total population by 25%. Success, however, was ephemeral. Disaster struck one of the relocated herds in 1988 when domestic sheep strayed into their habitat, infecting and killing all of them.

Then came a nasty surprise. A booming mountain lion population devastated both native and reestablished herds. Again, the species was on the verge of vanishing. Besides killing them outright, lions imperiled them by scaring them out of critical winter ranges. To avoid lions overrunning traditional warmer, lower elevation foraging grounds, bighorns stayed in high altitude Sierra wilderness and died from starvation or by avalanche. The trade-off for safety came at a huge cost. Biologists know that predators and prey typically maintain a balance in intact ecosystems. But all bets are off when trying to restore a small, very fragile population in a disturbed habitat.

The California mountain lion bounty program ended in 1963, and sport hunting was banned in 1972. Throughout the 1980s the lion population skyrocketed during the bighorn restoration program. Ultimately, in 1990 California voters passed Prop. 117 which protected lions from being hunted even by Fish and Game officials unless they damaged personal property (livestock, pets, etc.) or were deemed a public safety threat. Eight years later, two-thirds of Sierra wild sheep were dead. The 100 remaining bighorns were spread thinly among seven bands, some of which were solely females. With such low numbers, the tiny bands were once again tip-toeing on the edge of extinction.

Biologists can now relocate or kill lions that threaten wild sheep survival. Lynn Sadler of the Mountain Lion Foundation that pushed the 1990 initiative to protect the big cats supported the designation and funding. She was in agreement regarding the immediate need to relieve pressure on bighorns. Sadler also added, however, that predators must not be eliminated from the ecosystem. Said she, "we're kidding ourselves if we think we can create a zoo out there and protect a species forever."

True enough. Endangered status and selective lion removal by no means assure wild sheep survival because their numbers are dangerously low. Agency personnel recognize that too much predator control may create irreversible disturbances in the food chain that could cascade through the ecosystem, leading to new problems in the future.

It's ironic that further acts of man may be the only way to reverse the devastation we humans have already caused through decades of our influence and habitat encroachment and destruction. Environmental crises like this certainly underline the wisdom in the old saying, "Mother Nature always bats last!"

Further Reading

Clark, Ginny, *Ansel Adams Wilderness*, Western Trails Publications, Lake Havasu City, AZ, 2001.

_____, *Guide to Highway 395*, Western Trails Publications, Lake Havasu City, AZ, 1997.

_____, *Mammoth-Mono Country*, Publishers Group West, Berkeley, CA 1989.

Davis, Reanne, Mark Davis, and Don Douglass, *Mountain Biking the Eastern Sierra's Best 100 Trails*, Mountain Biking Press, Anacortes, WA, 1997.

Durham, David L., *Place Names of California's Eastern Sierra, Including Death Valley*, Quill Driver/Word Dancer Press, Clovis, CA, 2001.

Farquhar, Francis, *History of the Sierra Nevada*, University of California Press, Berkeley, CA, 1965.

Giacomazzi, Sharon, *Trails and Tales of Yosemite and the Central Sierra*, Bored Feet Press, Mendocino, CA, 2004.

Hanna, Jim, *Lundy: Gem of the Eastern Sierra*, Gold Hill Publishing Co., Virginia City, NV, 1990.

Huegel, Tony, *Sierra Nevada Byways*, Wilderness Press, Berkeley, CA, 2001.

Irwin, Sue, *California's Eastern Sierra*, Cachuma Press, Los Olivos, CA, 1997.
This is my first choice for a dynamic overview and precise understanding of the Eastern Sierra. Stunning photographs and beautifully crafted language make this book a must for anyone interested in visiting this dramatic landscape.

Konigsmark, Ted, *Geologic Trips: Sierra Nevada*, GeoPress, Gualala, CA (Distributed by Bored Feet Press, Mendocino, CA), 2003.

Leaderbrand, Russ, *Exploring Eastern Sierra Byways, Vol. VI: Owens Valley*, Westways, Los Angeles, 1972.

Mitchell, Roger, *High Sierra SUV Trails, Volume I, The East Side*, Track and Trail Publications, Oakhurst, CA, 2002.

Morey, Kathy, *Hot Showers, Soft Beds and Dayhikes in the Sierra*, Wilderness Press, Berkeley, CA 1996.

Parr, Barry, *Hiking the Sierra Nevada*, Globe Pequot Press, Guilford, CT, 1999.

Peattie, Donald Culross, *A Natural History of Western Trees*, Houghton Mifflin, Boston, 1950.

Roper, Steve, *The Climber's Guide to the High Sierra*, Sierra Club Books, San Francisco, 1976.

Schaffer, Jeffrey, *Yosemite National Park*, Wilderness Press, Berkeley, CA, 1997.

Schlenz, Mark, *Exploring the Eastern Sierra: California and Nevada*, Companion Press, Bishop, CA, 2003.

Secor, R. J.., *The High Sierra Peaks, Passes and Trails*, The Mountaineers, Seattle, 1999.

Smith, Genny, *Deepest Valley: Guide to Owens Valley*, Live Oak Press, Palo Alto, CA, 1995.

_____, *Mammoth Lakes Sierra*, Live Oak Press, Palo Alto, CA, 2006.

Spring, Vicky, *100 Hikes in California's Central Sierra and Coast Range*, The Mountaineers, Seattle, 1997.

Whitehill, Karen and Terry, *Best Short Hikes in California's Northern Sierra*, The Mountaineers, Seattle, 1990.

_____, *Best Short Hikes in California's Southern Sierra*, The Mountaineers, Seattle, 1999.

Winnett, Thomas and Jason, Lyn Haber, and Kathy Morey, *Sierra North*, Wilderness Press, Berkeley, CA, 1997.

Winnett, Thomas and Jason, Lyn Haber, Kathy Morey, *Sierra South*, Wilderness Press, 2001.

Wuerthner, George, *California's Wilderness Areas: The Complete Guide, Volume 1: Mountains and Coastal Range*s, Westcliffe Publishers, Englewood, CO, 1997.

Illustrations

continued from page 8

Index

About the Author

Sharon Giacomazzi is a Sierra hiker who happens to be an avid history buff and born storyteller. Sharon's love affair with the Sierra Nevada began early, as soon as she learned to walk. She grew up on a large ranch in the foothills below Kings Canyon National Park. When Sharon wasn't asleep or in school, she wandered the hills, wild and free, on foot or horseback. Mountain life got into her blood and stayed, even during years away at college and in the city earning a living as a teacher.

The urban setting always made Sharon feel like an alien, a stranger trapped in a strange land. Finally, in 1980, after 22 years of teaching, she decided to go home to the mountains where her spirit could be nurtured by the Sierra's natural rhythms and cycles.

Sharon bought property close to Yosemite and reconnected with her sense of place and her spiritual home. After building her house, she created ways to eke out a modest living, then began walking, and she hasn't stopped.

In the past 28 years, Sharon has trekked more than 8400 miles in the Sierra Nevada. She has been an outings leader for several environmental organizations and community colleges, as well as leader of her own history hikes. She has read and re-read scores of history books about the Sierra, finding they tremendously enriched her hiking experiences. Treading a trail is certainly rewarding, but Sharon found it a bit one dimensional. Knowing each place's background and nuances takes a hiker to another level of intimacy that is very gratifying.

Sharon started writing about the trails and tales of the Sierra Nevada in 1992. Like walking, once she got going she couldn't stop. Since then, her articles have appeared regularly in the *Yosemite Highway Herald* newspaper and *Sierra Heritage* and *California Explorer* magazines. Much to her amazement and delight, she encountered many people eager for something more than just a hiking guide to get them from point A to B. They wanted some 'meat with their potatoes," as one reader chose to put it. Following that suggestion, Sharon's first book, *Trails & Tales of Yosemite & Central Sierra* was published in 2001 and has been wildly successful.

Sharon loves to hike and write about her adventures. Like John Muir, she too feels blessed when she can entice someone to get out there and mingle with the rest of the food chain and 'taste the tonic of wilderness'.

The mountains are calling, and I must go.

~ John Muir

About Bored Feet

www.boredfeet.com

We began Bored Feet in 1986 to publish *The Hiker's hip pocket Guide to the Mendocino Coast*. We've grown our company by presenting the most accurate guidebooks for California, including the award-winning series, *Hiking the California Coastal Trail* and Sharon Giacomazzi's great Sierra guides. Thank you for supporting quality independent publishing with your purchase, helping us to bring you more information about gorgeous and fascinating California. We love to hear your feedback about this or any of our products.

Updates for several of our books are available at our website, **www.boredfeet.com**, where you can easily order any and all of our great books and maps. You also can get updates by sending us your name and address on a stamped envelope, specifying your areas of interest.

We offer quick (standard shipping) and lightning fast (rush) order service for the more than 180 books and 140 maps we carry about California and the West. If you prefer a catalog to ordering online, please call us. To order items, go to www.boredfeet.com, or send name, address / check or money order, or call us at one of the phone numbers below.

Trails & Tales of Yosemite & the Central Sierra	Sharon Giacomazzi	$ 17.50
Exploring Eastern Sierra Canyons: Sonora Pass to Pine Creek	Sharon Giacomazzi	15.50
Exploring Eastern Sierra Canyons: Bishop to Lone Pine	Sharon Giacomazzi	16.00
Geologic Trips: Sierra Nevada	Ted Konigsmark	17.50
Geologic Trips: San Francisco & the Bay Area	Ted Konigsmark	13.95
Hiking the CA Coastal Trail, Vol. 1: Oregon to Monterey, 2nd ed.	Lorentzen & Nichols	19.50
Hiking the CA Coastal Trail, Vol. 2: Monterey to Mexico	Lorentzen & Nichols	19.00
Day Trips with a Splash: Swimming Holes of California	Pancho Doll	19.95
Great Day Hikes in & around Napa Valley, 3rd edition	Ken Stanton	16.00
Napa Valley Picnic: A CA Wine Country Travel Companion	Jack Burton & Ken Stanton	15.00
Sonoma Picnic: A CA Wine Country Travel Companion	Jack Burton	15.00
Mendocino Coast Glove Box Guide: Lodgings Eateries, Sights, History, 3rd. edition	Bob Lorentzen	17.50
Hiker's hip pocket Guide to the Mendocino Coast, 3rd ed.	Bob Lorentzen	15.00
Hiker's hip pocket Guide to the Humboldt Coast, 2nd ed.	Bob Lorentzen	15.00
Hiker's hip pocket Guide to Sonoma County, 3rd ed.	Bob Lorentzen	16.00
Hiker's hip pocket Guide to the Mendocino Highlands, 2nd ed.	Bob Lorentzen	17.00

Please add $4 shipping for orders under $30, $6 over $30 ($7 / 11 for rush).
For shipping to a California address, please add 8.25% sales tax.
Prices subject to change without notice.

BORED FEET PRESS
www.boredfeet.com
P.O. BOX 1832
MENDOCINO, CA 95460
888-336-6199
707-964-6629